1 3 4 6

On Defining the Proper Name

John Algeo

University of Florida Press

Gainesville • 1973

Library of Congress Cataloging in Publication Data

Algeo, John   1930–
    On defining the proper name.

    (University of Florida humanities monograph no. 41)
    Bibliography: p.   ·
    1. Names, English.   2. English language—
Semantics.   3. English language—Noun.
I. Title.   II. Series: Florida.   University,
Gainesville.   University of Florida monograph.
Humanities, no. 41.
PE1578.A2A5   428′.1   73–9849
ISBN 0–8130–0410–1

Foreword

SOME YEARS AGO at an annual meeting of the American Name Society, one of the papers was followed by discussion of uncommon acerbity. As an organization in which professionalism has not yet replaced gentleman-scholarship, the Name Society's meetings are usually marked by polite exchanges springing from a determination to find interest and significance in whatever paper is read before it. On this occasion, however, tempers strayed, if they were not quite lost, and there was a sharp exchange of words over the question of whether or not the subject matter of one of the papers could appropriately be called "names." The disagreement arose chiefly from the fact that those involved had different, although not clearly formulated, notions of what a name is. Because they started from different general positions, there was little hope of their arriving at the same particular end.

Quarrels often spring from unclear or conflicting definitions, so the groundwork of any study must be the definition of its object. In recent years onomastics has had several theoretical isagoges that focus on the problem of defining names, for example, those by Farhang Zabeeh (1968), Holger Sørensen (1963), and Ernst Pulgram (1954); the oldest, and in many ways still the best, of these is Sir Alan Gardiner's study, originally published in 1940 and only slightly revised for its second edition (1954).* Although the views expressed in the present study are closest to those of Sir Alan, I believe he was led astray by an inadequate view of the structure of language.

In this study, the assumption is made that language must be accounted for as a series of interconnected but autonomous levels (for which the terms stratum and plane are used interchangeably in the following pages). This work is, however, no more an ex-

*References begin on p. 89.

plicitly stratificational treatment of names than it is a systemic treatment or a transformational one. Its conclusions are not dependent on any particular theory or formalism, although it does assume that language is most adequately accounted for as an interlocking set of discrete systems. From this standpoint, one of the chief faults of most prior treatments of names is the assumption, often unconscious, that names are a unified monostratal phenomenon. The main goal of this study is to correct that apparent misassumption.

I am grateful to a number of persons for their help in the preparation of the study: Robert H. West and James B. Colvert, past and present chairmen of the English Department of the University of Georgia, for support during the summer of 1972 to complete the writing; Robert H. Longshore for help in providing clerical assistance; April Maddox for her skillful translation of the manuscript into typescript; and a number of persons who read the study and provided valuable criticism, especially Adele S. Algeo, O. C. Dean, James B. McMillan, and Thomas Pyles. I have benefitted greatly from the suggestions, examples, corrections, and objections they offered; the errors and misinterpretations that obstinately remain are mine alone.

J.A.

Contents

1. The Problem of Defining the Term *Name*   1
2. Orthographical and Phonological Names   14
3. Morphosyntactic Names   20
4. Referential Names   42
5. Semantic Names: The Degree of Meaning   53
6. Semantic Names: The Kind of Meaning   68
References   89

1

The Problem of Defining the Term *Name*

THE STUDY of names is coeval in the Western world with the study of language itself. Indeed, it might be said that European linguistics is the child of onomastics, for the oldest extant Greek work on language is Plato's *Cratylus*, an inquiry into the relationship between words and things, in particular whether names are in some sense naturally connected to those who bear them or are assigned by convention merely. The dialog begins with an argument between two friends of Socrates, Cratylus and Hermogenes, about the latter's name, in which Cratylus maintains that *Hermogenes* cannot possibly be his companion's true name. He insists there must be a natural appropriateness of the name to the thing it designates; however, *Hermogenes* means 'born of Hermes,' the god of cleverness, money, and good fortune, and is therefore clearly inappropriate for such a dull, impecunious, and wretched fellow. The opening argument of the *Cratylus* is, to be sure, a ponderous, academic joke that Cratylus is using to "psych out" his companion, the more easily to get the better of him in the serious discussion that is to follow. Behind the etymological jest about Hermogenes' name, however, there lies the serious question of whether names in general can be said to have meaning or whether they are empty labels for things. The debate between the naturalists, who saw the name as revelatory of the thing named, and the conventionalists, who saw the name as an arbitrary designation, continued through the following centuries and in somewhat altered terms is still very much alive today. In onomastics, as in much else, it can be said that there are few new answers and no new questions. The study of names began in the ancient world, and if since then we have seen farther, it is, as Newton observed and Bernard of Chartres before him, because we stand upon the shoulders of giants (Merton 1965).

The history of the grammatical analysis of proper names, whose beginnings can be seen in the *Cratylus*, is part of the long and tangled story of the development of part of speech systems in the European tradition (Michael 1970; Robins 1967). Within that tradition, proper names seem first to have been recognized as a distinct linguistic category by the Stoic grammarians. Earlier, the undifferentiated mix of syntax, rhetoric, and logic, out of which the study of language was to crystalize in several directions over the centuries, made do with a single term, *onoma*, where later grammarians would want at least three: *name, noun,* and *subject*. Thus Plato, in both the *Cratylus* (399B, 425A) and the *Sophist* (262A–263D), uses *onoma* indifferently for *name* or *noun* or, as the designation of one of the two main parts of a sentence, for *subject*. Part of the Stoic improvement in discrimination was to set up the *onoma* 'proper name' and the *prosegoria* 'common noun' as major word classes, based on the semantic contrast between "individual quality" and "common quality" (Robins 1966:12). The two sorts of words were regrouped as subclasses of the same major part of speech by Dionysius Thrax. In his short *Art of Grammar*, probably the most influential textbook ever written, Dionysius says there are two kinds of *onoma*: the *onoma kyrion*, which is applied to an individual, and the *onoma prosegorikon*, which is applied commonly (Davidson 1874:331, 333). In this distinction, as in many others, Dionysius set the fashion for the multitudes who followed him. The two works that were instrumental in transmitting Dionysian grammar to the Middle Ages and the Renaissance, Priscian's *Institutiones Grammaticae* and Donatus' *Ars Minor*, echo the Greek grammarian in subdividing nouns as *nomen proprium* and *nomen appellativum*, the name respectively of one and of many. Priscian expresses the difference thus: "Appellativum naturaliter commune est multorum . . . ut 'animal,' 'corpus.' . . . Proprium vero naturaliter uniuscuiusque privatam substantiam et qualitatem significat et in rebus est individuis, quas philosophi atomos vocant, ut 'Plato,' 'Socrates' " (Keil 1864:2.58–59).

The classical beginnings of onomastic study provide in outline the structure followed by both grammarians and philosophers to the present time. Names are a kind of noun, a product of the first subcategorization of nouns into two groups: proper and common. Proper nouns are stated to have individual application, and common nouns general application, being the names respectively of one and of many. The only significant departure from Dionysian grammar in the ancient world was that of Varro, who in the *De Lingua Latina* (8.45) set up a rigorously formal part of speech system and subdivided nouns into four classes: *vocabula* 'common nouns' like *shield* or *sword*, *provocabula* 'pro-common-nouns' like *who* or *what*, *nomina* 'proper nouns' like *Romulus* or *Remus*, and *pronomina* 'pro-proper-nouns' like *this* or *that*. Although he is not explicit about the criteria for distinguishing his subclasses, it is clear that Varro did not have recourse to the individual-general or one-many contrast in his analysis. Rather the principle that distinguishes the two *nomen*-classes from the two *vocabulum*-classes is quite clearly the feature of definiteness, to be discussed in chapter 3. In this, as in much of his grammatical thought, Varro shows a refreshing originality, which was not to be emulated by those who came after him. The Dionysian approach has dominated onomastic study for well over two thousand years. Not until the last hundred years has it been seriously challenged. In these latter days, however, several new views have been advanced, but none generally accepted, so that in the present state of onomastic study there is no consensus on how to define the object of the discipline.

In view of the fact that names have been studied in a continuous tradition for twenty-four hundred years or so, it is perhaps remarkable that there is now little agreement about what a name is. There are, of course, many definitions. That, indeed, is the problem. The term *name* has been defined in diverse, often mutually incompatible ways; as a result, some arguments about names spring from inconsistent or unclear notions of what is being discussed. Some notion of the variety of things that find their way under the umbrella of onomastics can be gathered from the more than five hundred entries in Witkowski's (1964) glossary of German onomastic terms, most of which can easily be matched with English equivalents.

Part of the present uncertainty about what counts as a name and what does not is due to the long dominance of the classical tradition and its unthinking acceptance by succeeding generations of students. As Brøndal (1948:58) has observed, "La notion de nom a, comme celle de nombre, semblé si bien connue et si immédiatement compréhensible à la plupart des grammairiens qu'ils ne se sont pas donnés la peine de lui consacrer de définition." But the notion of a name, far from being obvious, is so unclear that one theorist (Utley

1963:150) has questioned whether it would not be better in general to deal with various kinds of names, such as place names and personal names, which he believes can be defined more easily, and to leave the existence of a unified category of proper names an unresolved issue. However, as long as there is no clear sense of what the term *proper name* means, onomatologists are in the position of not knowing what they are talking about. This is, as Quine (1963: 47) has noted, not an untenable position, although certainly an uncomfortable one.

Part of the confusion about names is attributable to onomastics itself, for the study of names has in practice embraced two rather different objects: proper names and terminologies. A terminology, also called a nomenclature, is a semantically coherent set of expressions used to designate the members of a class of objects, activities, or so forth; it is the group of terms used in talking about a particular subject; it is the words, usually common nouns, that form a lexical set in the sense of Halliday (1961:276). Given the uncertainty about proper names, the distinction between them and a terminology can be illustrated more readily than defined. Reference to horses will do as well as any subject. On the one hand, in dealing with horsey matters, there are such terminologies as are exemplified by the terms *palomino* versus *pinto*, *dray horse* versus *carriage horse* or *saddle horse*, *mudder* versus *trotter* or *charger*, and *stallion* versus *mare* or *gelding*. On the other hand, there are proper names like *Bucephalus, Black Beauty, Man o' War, Dobbin, Pegasus*, and *Seabiscuit*. It is obvious that the two objects of onomastic study are of different kinds, even though they are both called "names" and sometimes overlap. The overlap can be seen in the proper names for city streets, which may involve a terminology by which streets are distinguished from avenues according to the direction they run, north-south or east-west. Even when the choice of term is not predictable from the compass, common nouns like *street, avenue, boulevard, lane, road, circle, way, path, alley,* and *terrace* constitute a terminology whose members may enter into proper names. Similarly, personal names are one kind of proper name, but they include titles like *Mr., Mrs., Miss, Ms., Dr.,* and *Rt. Rev.,* which form a terminology. Personal names themselves may be based on a terminology, like those derived from the days of the week. Robinson Crusoe's Friday, who was so called "for the memory of the time," and Tuesday Weld, for whatever reason she was so called, come to mind, although better examples are the African day-names that turned up among the black population of the New World (DeCamp 1967). Originally they were personal names that indicated the sex of the bearer and the day of the week on which he was born: *Quasheba* 'Sunday,' *Juba* 'Monday,' *Beneba* 'Tuesday,' *Cubba* 'Wednesday,' *Abba* 'Thursday,' *Phibba* 'Friday,' and *Mimba* 'Saturday,' to cite the female forms.

In general, however, the distinction between proper names and terminologies is clear. Although proper names and the common nouns that make up a terminology are both called names—in ordinary language and in technical onomastic use—this study is concerned only with the former, and therefore *name* can hereafter be understood unambiguously as short for *proper name*. Terminologies are no less legitimate subjects of onomastic study, but they are not under study here.

There are other uses of *name* in particular "registers," or areas of discourse, with which this study will not deal but whose existence needs to be recognized to avoid possible confusion. For example, in the law there is a special kind of name, the trademark or brand name (Berle and de Camp 1959:450–78); *Frigidaire* is a trademark name, sometimes used illegally in a generic sense, whereas *refrigerator* has never been a trademark and *Kelvinator* is so exclusively. A trademark may be integrated so thoroughly into the vocabulary as the generic term for an object that few speakers are aware of its special legal status. Familiarity with the trademark and lack of any convenient generic term to compete with it account for the fact that a brand name like *zipper* is taken over by the general vocabulary. Alternative generic terms, such as *interlocking slide fastener*, are too bureaucratic in their associations. They sound like governmental gobbledegook and are so treated by the ordinary man, who knows enough to call a zipper a zipper. Similarly *aspirin*, although originally a trademark, has passed completely into the public domain, happily replacing *acetyl spiraeic* (or *salicylic*) *acid* as the generic term.

In countries such as France, there are official lists of personal names which may include *Louis* but not *Lance*, thus giving one and not the other official status as a "name" (Ashley 1971). The motive behind governmental control of naming practices may be either to prevent the use of what are deemed unsuitable names or to encourage greater diversification of names for clarity of reference.

Thus governments have encouraged the disuse of names like *Coward, Hogg,* and *Krapp,* which has not, however, prevented them from being proudly borne by distinguished persons. When a French court forbade Gérard and Paulette Trognon to bestow their surname on their adopted son, on the grounds that *Trognon* 'stump, butt end' was a "nom ridicule" and would be "un handicap," Trognons throughout France rose up in their defense (*Time,* 11 September 1972, pp. 28–31). The need for variety impelled the Swedish government to draw up a list of 900,000 unique new surnames by having a computer randomly combine syllables (Landau 1967:16). The problem that the computer was intended to solve is that there are too few Scandinavian family names because many of them were originally patronyms, limited in variety by the small number of popular masculine given names on which they were based. Consequently a few names like *Olson, Hanson, Gustafson,* or *Swenson* occur with confusing frequency, even more so than comparable names like *Thompson, Johnson,* and *Jones* in British and American society. The convenience of the state is served by distinctness of its citizens' names.

Government efforts to control names have been widespread (Rennick 1970; Wolf-Rottkay 1971:238), although not always successful. They are, moreover, not limited to personal names; indeed in the United States, where there is relatively little governmental control of a person's name, official agencies are more likely to be concerned with place names. Long-established names of topographical features can be changed by government decree, as that of *Cape Canaveral* was to *Cape Kennedy,* although a successful change requires popular sympathy in support of it. When the federal Bureau of Land Management decided to change the name of *Whorehouse Meadows,* near Ontario, Oregon, originally named in honor of four working girls who entertained the sheepherders (according to a UPI dispatch in the Birmingham, Alabama, *Post Herald,* 4 December 1972, p. 3/2, a reference kindly supplied by James B. McMillan), local pride was mobilized and the Oregon state board for geographical names petitioned for a return to the traditional designation. Official sanction or disapproval can create a legal class of names or nonnames, but it does not necessarily affect popular naming practices, and it is with the latter rather than with official lists that this study is concerned.

In logic there are special uses of the term *name* that have little or nothing to do with its use in onomastics. It may be used, for example, in the sense 'that which names,' thus implying the existence of a named object (Quine 1960:180). In this use, any putative name for which there is no corresponding object cannot in fact be a name. In a different use, *name* or *proper name* may be alternative expressions for a *singular term*, by which use proper names would encompass not only *Sir Walter Scott* and *Chomolungma*, but also *the author of Waverley* and *the highest mountain in the world* (Church 1956:3–9).

Bertrand Russell made several important and influential statements about proper names (1918; 1948:72–84), which have in common that they characterize a special technical use of the term rather than describe what might be thought of as proper names in ordinary language. For Russell, proper names in a "logically perfect language" are words for particulars—for qualities and complexes of "compresent" qualities—the closest thing in ordinary language being words like *this* or *that*. Words like *Socrates* are not proper names at all, but "are really abbreviations for descriptions"; and therefore "proper names in the ordinary sense, if this is right, are misleading, and embody a false metaphysic," being the "ghosts of substances." Russell was careful to specify that his concern was a technical use of the term *name* and not the ordinary one; yet his statements about what ordinary names "really" are, if his technical use of the term "is right," certainly suggest the transcendence of an arbitrarily stipulated definition and an encroachment upon linguistic description. Russell seems to be exhibiting the Humpty-Dumpty syndrome, by which a definition that is first prescribed for a stipulated use is illegitimately extended to domains other than that for which it was defined and ends by masquerading as a description or a critique of actual use:

> "There's glory for you!"
> "I don't know what you mean by 'glory,'" Alice said.
> Humpty Dumpty smiled contemptuously. "Of course you don't—till I tell you. I meant 'there's a nice knock-down argument for you!'"
> "But 'glory' doesn't mean 'a nice knock-down argument,'" Alice objected.
> "When *I* use a word," Humpty Dumpty said, in rather a scornful tone, "it means just what I choose it to mean—neither more or less."

> "The question is," said Alice "whether you *can* make words
> mean so many different things."
> "The question is," said Humpty Dumpty, "which is to be
> master—that's all." (Carroll 1871:268–69)

Humpty Dumpty, the arch-egghead, was playing a game according to his own idiosyncratic rules. Alice, in her commonsensical way, assumed that everybody has to use the public rules. Opposite Russell's Humpty Dumpty, Sir Alan Gardiner has filled the role of Alice in his analysis of the logician's views, which he called "assuredly the most fantastic theory of proper names that has ever come to birth" (1954:57). Sir Alan was, to be sure, aware that Russell was talking logic and not onomastics, but inasmuch as Russell himself blurred the distinction, the Alicean response is not wholly inappropriate. Logically proper names, as Russell has characterized them, simply do not exist in ordinary language. In terms of Strawson's (1959:9) distinction between descriptive metaphysics, which "is content to describe the actual structure of our thought about the world," and revisionary metaphysics, which "is concerned to produce a better structure," it is clear that Russell is a revisionist. Linguistics, of which onomastics is a subdiscipline, has much to learn from other studies like philosophy that deal to some extent with the same subject matter; but because all linguistics is primarily a descriptive study and only secondarily a revisionary one and because it approaches the subject with its own assumptions and aims, it maintains its autonomy from other language-oriented disciplines (Wells 1954). With the special uses of the term *proper name* in logic and other branches of philosophy, this study will not be concerned.

Stipulated definitions are not, however, restricted to logicians. Brøndal's study (1948:92) of the parts of speech, which aims at a set of definitions universally applicable, proposes an a priori concept of *proper noun* that excludes from the class all morphemically complex items like *Eiffel Tower, New-port, Eng-land, Cam-bridge,* and even *Ital-y* and *Turk-ey.* It likewise excludes words that are homonymous with common appellatives, such as *Grace, Smith,* or presumably the *Wash.* From the standpoint of any ordinary concept of *name,* these exclusions are arbitrary and unwarranted. For Brøndal (1948:145), an example of the proper name par excellence is French *ce*: "Le français possède aussi un mot qui désigne exclusivement un objet déterminé (*R*), concept qui définit le nom propre. Ce nom propre universel est *ce*, ancien pronom démonstratif (*RD*) qui a perdu toute trace d'indétermination (*D*)." The notion that French *ce* is a pure or universal example of a proper name has some affinity with Russell's view that the closest thing normal language has to logically proper names is a word like *this* or *that*. The view is, however, no more congenial to descriptive study when advanced by a Danish linguist than when advanced by an English philosopher.

In general the concern of this study will be linguistic forms that can be called proper names in ordinary language, rather than in any of the technical or restricted uses of the kinds mentioned above. Moreover, its concern will be the ordinary use of ordinary language rather than out-of-the-way or idiosyncratic uses (Ryle 1953:108–12). The emphasis on "ordinary language" should not, however, be taken to imply either that this study is based on the Ordinary Language school of philosophy or that it will investigate all the ways the term *name* is ordinarily used. The first would be too restrictive since Ordinary Language philosophy is still a kind of philosophy, not a kind of grammar; the second would be too loose because *name* is freely used in a great many divergent ways in everyday language. The center of study will be those things that most grammarians and most students of onomastics have agreed to call *names*. The purpose of the study is to survey some ways of characterizing that class of things and of defining the term *name* for onomastic purposes. In doing so, a major concern will be the distinction between universals of naming and the facts of a particular language. Language-specific facts about names are interesting and important for the study of the individual languages, but linguistic universals of naming are what must be the ultimate concern of any study of onomastics. The focus of this study is on proper names as they are used in English, but a pervasive question is whether the English treatment of names is idiosyncratic or embodies a general fact about naming practice.

It is commonly accepted that there are universals of naming—specifically, that all languages provide for a class of items that can be called proper names, that in all cultures there are events that are identified as "namings" (Pulgram 1954:3; Hockett 1958:311), and further that names are a kind of noun in any language with a class of words that can be called nouns (presumably any language whatever). Those views have not gone unchallenged. Thus Hamp (1956:347) suggests that "it is probably only our typical West-European thought patterns that lead us to confuse, or single out, noun as the partner for name; if we were Semites or Algonquians, we might well seek to distinguish names from predications or verbs." Hacking (1968) has argued that there can be and very probably are natural languages without particulars—among which we must presumably include proper names—citing studies by American anthropological linguists of Kwakiutl and Nootka, which are supposed to have strikingly un-European structures.

Whether names are to be considered a kind of noun, and therefore to be contrasted with other kinds of nouns, may depend on whether we have in mind their syntax, that is, their external grammatical relations with other items in some larger construction, or their morphology, that is, the internal grammar of their own structure. That names, grammatically considered, function like nouns within the sentence and are thus syntactically nouns is very likely to be a universal truth. That names are made up according to the same patterns that nouns are is, on the contrary, a very uncertain universal. Indeed, in chapter 3 it will be seen that the second generalization does not hold even for English, so there is no need to look to exotica to prove it wrong. Names are not always morphologically nouns (although it would also be possible to argue that nouns are not always morphologically nouns either). However, that fact still leaves open the validity of the weaker assumption that "not only name-bearing, but also namebuilding is a universal human practice, with the same elementary rules everywhere, just as human language is basically the same physical and nervous performance of human speech production and comprehension, regardless of the multitude and variety of languages" (Pulgram 1954:20).

Whether a natural human language without terms for particulars in its surface structure—that is, a natural language with the form of the predicate calculus—exists or might be expected to exist is less certain than Hacking would have it. Examples from American Indian languages like Kwakiutl and Nootka have long, but unconvincingly, been offered as proof that "Standard Average European" (as Whorf called it) and Amerindian tongues present radically different views of the world and everything in it. The problem is that to compare the Weltanschauung of the two languages, one must be paraphrased into the other, and paraphrases are tricky things. Quite ordinary expressions in quite ordinary languages, including English itself, can be paraphrased in a way that would make them seem very un-European, and exotic tongues like Kwakiutl can be translated in a way that makes them the very Doppelgänger of any Indo-European language. Paraphrases lack conviction. What is needed is a native command of both languages coupled with the linguistic sophistication to analyze, contrast, and interpret the two systems. So far such a happy conjunction of competence and ability has not enfleshed itself in many persons. And until it does, some caution is in order in accepting an analysis of exotic languages that shows them to depart from what, on other grounds, we might reasonably assume to be universal features of human language.

Even though naming is in some sense "instinctual," there is no reason to expect we can ever identify the "instinct" that underlies it. Efforts to do so, like that of Feldman (1959), who believes names to be an expression of antagonism toward the named object and the use of names to be an aggressive act, are examples of psychoanalysis gone to seed. It is, however, not too much to hope that some universally valid criteria for defining names can be found. If such criteria suggest an explanation for the universality, so much the better. But having no explanation is better than having a misleading one.

The fact that names are universal in human language (assuming it to be a fact) need not imply any phylogenetic priority for them. The view popular among some writers (Jespersen 1922:438; Christophersen 1939:64; Pulgram 1954:6) that proper names were the oldest kind of noun or even the original kind of word is probably due to an uncritical acceptance of a romantic view of the savage as a simple, uncomplex soul, given to concrete thinking rather than abstraction and preoccupied with the immediate present and sense perceptions. The myth of the simple savage has also given rise to fables about languages that consist of no more than two hundred words, which are on a par with the just-so fable of some dawn-man wandering through the primeval forest bestowing proper names on the animals, trees, and rocks, and only gradually generalizing those names to stand for any similar object, thereby discovering the concept of species. It is, of course, beside the point that the Greek term *onoma kyrion*, from which our *proper name* ultimately derives, seems originally to have meant 'name, properly speaking, properly so called, in the proper sense of the word,' thus leaving common names as second-class members of the part of speech. Despite its etymology, _etymology_ provides no insight into the "true" or "real" meaning of words. What the Greeks thought about proper names is an important part of the history of such words, but it tells nothing about their origin, for Delphi was a long way from the dawn-forest, and Chrysippus the Stoic, who is reputed to have originated the grammatical term, was many a generation removed from the primeval name-giver.

The romantic view, which long antedates its twentieth-century proponents cited above, was challenged before them by Max Müller (1891:512–19), who held the opposite view, namely that language originated in general ideas expressed by general terms and only later were some of them individualized and specialized into proper names. If we are forced to choose sides in this dichotomy, it can be said in support of Max Müller that the way children learn language seems to offer more support for his view than for the romantic one. Children are said to generalize through recognizing likenesses more readily than to particularize through differentiation. If ontogeny recapitulates linguistic phylogeny, we might suppose with Max Müller that languages began with something like the roots he favored, expressive of general notions. However, he himself seems to have suspected the dichotomy, for he cites Sir William Hamilton's *Lectures on Metaphysics* to the effect that children, and presumably also dawn-man, at first command neither general terms nor individual ones, in our sense, but rather a single undifferentiated sort of term, which seems vague and confused to us, but out of which eventually develop the categories we expect. There is much to recommend this view, in which neither the proper nor the common name has any natural priority, historical or grammatical, over the other. Being correlative notions, it is not until proper names and appellatives both exist that there can be any contrast between them.

Universals of naming, whatever they may be, are necessarily reflected in the structure and use of particular languages, and so it is with the latter that study must begin. A number of criteria have been suggested for proper names in English, among which these are the most prominent:

ORTHOGRAPHIC: Proper names are capitalized.

MORPHOSYNTACTIC:	Proper names have no plural forms.
	Proper names are used without articles.
	Proper names do not accept restrictive modifiers.
REFERENTIAL:	Proper names refer to single unique individuals.
SEMANTIC:	Proper names do not impute any qualities to the objects designated and are therefore meaningless.
	Proper names have a distinctive form of definition that includes a citation of their expression.

In the following chapters, all of the foregoing criteria, and some additional related ones, will be examined for their appropriateness to the way *proper name* is ordinarily used, for their mutual compatibility, and for their universality. In the process it will become clear that what they define is not a single, natural class of words, but rather a number of different sorts of names only roughly coterminous with one another. To distinguish these items from one another, the following terminological distinctions will be made: on the orthographic level, there are ORTHOGRAPHIC NAMES or CAPITALIZED WORDS versus UNCAPITALIZED WORDS; on the morphosyntactic level, there are PROPER NOUNS versus COMMON NOUNS; on the referential level, there are SINGULAR TERMS versus GENERAL TERMS; on the semantic level, there are PROPER NAMES or simply NAMES versus COMMON NAMES or APPELLATIVES. To talk about a "name" in the abstract is to run the risk of hypostatizing a linguistic fiction. What names are depends on whether we are concerned with semantics, reference, grammar, phonology, or orthography. It depends also on whether we are concerned with the universals of naming or with the facts of a particular language.

2

Orthographical and Phonological Names

O N WHAT is the most accessible level of language, the expression plane, it is conceivable that names might be characteristically marked in any of the substances by which language is expressed, most particularly in writing or speech. And, indeed, capitalization in English writing is often cited as a mark of the proper name. In the standard orthography there is a class of written words that regularly begin with a capital letter, regardless of the position they happen to occupy within the sentence. This class of orthographic names (as they may be called) correlates roughly with the class of proper names defined in other ways, but the correlation is not exact.

Automobile names like *Ford* or *Volkswagen* are capitalized in all uses. When they are names of the companies, they are grammatically proper nouns because they are regularly used without articles, but when they refer to the company's product—an automobile— they are grammatically common since they then require an article. Compare "Onassis sold the Ford and bought a Volkswagen" with "Onassis sold Ford and bought Volkswagen." Product names like a *Ford*, a *Volkswagen*, a *Kodak*, and a *Frigidaire*, are grammatically common by every morphosyntactic criterion that has been proposed to distinguish proper from common nouns, including the three mentioned at the end of chapter 1. They are freely pluralized: "Fords are selling well this year"; "He owns two Fords." They are used with articles, and indeed require articles under exactly the same conditions as any common noun: "He has a Ford/car, but the Ford/car is second-hand," not *"He has Ford/car, but Ford/car is second-hand." They accept restrictive modifiers without difficulty: "The last Ford he bought was a lemon." The fact that the words in question are trademarks is, as has already been observed, not relevant to their linguistic status, although the fact that they are

14

grammatically common nouns may be a contributory factor to the ease with which trademarks pass into generic use when other conditions favor such a shift. The fact that a word is capitalized is no guide to its status as a proper name on other levels.

Neither is the lack of capitalization a reliable clue to a word's grammar. Thus, the word *base* in the expression *first base, second base, third base* is always lowercase. Grammatically and semantically, however, it has two strikingly different uses. One use is for any of the four stations at the corners of the infield, in which case the term is grammatically common according to the criteria already mentioned: "a base, bases, the base he is on." The other use is for a particular one of the three stations other than home plate, in which case the term is grammatically proper, rejecting the definite article, as in "The runner was out at second (base)," for which *"The runner was out at the second (base)" would be at best odd and unidiomatic. The contrast between these two uses of *base* can be seen in sentences like "First base is the first base a runner touches," or "The first bases he stole were third base and second base." Other items like *first base* and *second base* are *top banana, second tenor, south* and *dummy* in bridge, and *fullback* as in "A quarterback rarely plays fullback." Such terms are not often thought of as proper nouns, chiefly perhaps because they are not capitalized, but they satisfy the grammatical criteria for properness and thereby demonstrate that some grammatically proper words are written in lower case.

The examples so far cited show that items can be treated alike on the orthographic level, either capitalized or lower-cased, although they belong to different grammatical and semantic classes. The following examples will show that some items belonging to the same grammatical or semantic classes are treated in different ways on the orthographic level. The names of the planets, *Mars, Venus, Pluto,* and so on, are always capitalized, whereas the name of the third planet, *earth,* is usually spelled with an initial lower case, although it would seem to be semantically as much a proper name as the others. To be sure, the planet name *Earth* may be capitalized, but it also may not, whereas *Mars, Venus,* and so forth would be quite unusual with lowercase spellings. Similarly *Caucasian,* a noun indicative of race, is regularly capitalized, whereas the noun *white,* in the same racial sense, is regularly lowercase. Both words are grammatically common nouns.

Caucasian is typical of grammatically common nouns synchronically derived from proper names, in this case from *Caucasus* or *Caucasia*. Other examples are *Parisian* from *Paris*, *Chinese* from *China*, *Trotskyite* from *Trotsky*, and *Michigander* from *Michigan*. Such words are proper orthographically but not syntactically. For some words, capitalization serves incidentally to distinguish homonyms: *Democrat* versus *democrat*, *Shaker* versus *shaker*, and *Odd Fellow* versus *odd fellow*. The orthographic contrast with homonyms is, however, neither diachronic explanation nor synchronic justification for their capitalization, which is to be found rather in their connection with proper names like the *Democratic Party* and the *Independent Order of Odd Fellows*. Finally, some words are sporadically capitalized honoris causa: "a Committee meeting," "a future Convention," "the present Administration," "Transformational-Generative grammar," and recently *Black* as a racial term.

There is a good deal of variation in the capitalization of some of the words cited above, but that variation is itself evidence of the poor correlation of orthography with grammatical or semantic facts. The Chicago *Manual of Style* (1969:147–94) devotes nearly fifty pages to rules for capitalization, chiefly in an effort to resolve the problematical cases, and actual unedited usage shows a great deal more variation than style guides suggest. Variation exists partly because the rules for capitalization are sui generis, rather than reflections of systematic distinctions made on other levels of the language.

Grammarians often assume a greater correlation between capitalization and grammatically proper nouns than in fact exists. Thus Pulgram (1954:37), in one of the more extreme statements of the kind, urged his readers to "notice the prevalent spelling practice in English today: names of apples with majuscules—they are strictly proper names to the great majority of speakers; names of automobiles with majuscules—they, also, are proper names, associated with the name of the producers or the factory, they are trademarks; but the names of breeds of dogs are mostly spelled with minuscules—because they have, in general usage, long ago ceased to be proper names and have become, through their importance to humans, familiar general nouns." He goes on to conclude that "in modern English the spelling actually is indicative of the usage of a word," but his argument might more precisely be said to be that the spelling determines whether a word is proper or common, for only on that basis is it possible to make sense of the idea that *Delicious* and *Datsun* are proper whereas *dachshund* is common.

Not many grammarians who have been influenced by American structuralism, with its insistence that language is speech and that writing is at best a derivative representation, would subscribe to the naïve assumption that what is capitalized is a proper name; but the opposite assumption, that majuscules are used for words that can be shown on syntactic or semantic grounds to be proper, has been made more or less explicitly. Thus Long (1969:109) suggests that "the honorific capital letters with which most proper names are begun are a tribute the written language pays to individuality," and Paul Roberts in one of his high school textbooks (1967:17) cautions the student, "Obviously we can't find out which nouns are proper ones by just noting which nouns are capitalized. . . . We should still have to ask ourselves how [the writer] knows which nouns to capitalize and which not." The assumption is that we can define proper nouns some other way—by their behavior with articles, for example—and that all nouns so defined will be capitalized. There may be pedagogical justification for such an assumption, made also by Quirk et al. (1972:160, 164), but it is not wholly accurate as a description of linguistic fact.

Gleason (1965:186) has made the valid and significant point that because the use of capitals in spelling has no phonological reference whatever, insofar as capitalization represents anything from another part of the linguistic system, it is grammatical information about the word class of proper nouns. But capitalization turns out to give relatively little information about any other level of language, for the orthography is an autonomous system with its own, often idiosyncratic, rules and has only an approximate correlation with syntax or anything else. Most but not all proper nouns are capitalized in English, and a great many things that certainly are not proper nouns are regularly capitalized. Present-day English has some words like *Chevrolet* that are usually capitalized, some like *Roman* that are often capitalized, some like *devil* that are occasionally capitalized, and some like *first base* that are rarely capitalized. Among the several reasons for a majuscule is that a word is thought to be "proper" in some way other than orthographical, although forms like *first base* and *earth* show that there are grammatically or semantically proper words that are written in minuscules.

It is also worth noting that the Modern English use of capitals is limited to a single état de langue. Proof of that obvious fact is that classical writing used only majuscules (or rather, that the minuscule-majuscule distinction did not appear until early medieval times) and that the post-classical use of majuscules has varied greatly. Thus Modern German begins all nouns with capitals whereas Old English used capitals only to begin sentences. German spells *Mann* with a capital, and Old English spelled *Alfred* all lowercase. In neither system does the use of majuscules define a class one can identify even approximately as proper names. Furthermore, other periods, other languages, and other writing systems have their own devices for identifying orthographic names. Thus, in the eighteenth century, proper names were often italicized. In the Initial Teaching Alphabet, the first letter is boldface. In the Shavian alphabet, proper names are preceded by a raised dot, and in the alphabet of the International Phonetic Association, by an asterisk. In hieroglyphic Egyptian, the cartouche set off royal names. In cuneiform, divine names were accompanied by a special identifying symbol as a determinative. And doubtless other devices have been used. Two things, however, are clear: written representation of names is a language-specific and highly variable matter; and the class of written names in present-day English is not the same as the class of grammatical or semantic names.

Indeed, the fact that English has any kind of written symbolization for "nameness" is remarkable, as Gleason has pointed out, because generally writing is more restricted in what it can signal than is speech; and English has no phonologically defined class of names, nor is it likely that many languages do. Still, it is conceivable that a language might indicate names by their sound. One artificial language, Loglan (developed by James Brown at the University of Florida in the 1960s), has proper names that can be recognized from their pronunciation, because they and they alone are polysyllabic words ending in a consonant. But in natural languages such phenomena must surely be rare. It has been reported by Harms (1968:13) that Finnish proper names are exempt from certain phonological rules affecting all common nouns. In that case there would seem to be a phonologically defined class of words that coincides at least partly with the class of semantic proper names, but it is doubtful that the correlation is exact.

It is, to be sure, well known that names often have a form at variance with what the general rules of historical sound change would lead us to expect from their etyma. Instances like *York* from *Eoforwic*, *Wooster* from *Worcester*, and *maudlin* from *Magdalene* are well known, but more parochial examples, like St. Louis' *Forest Park*, whose first word is locally pronounced to rime with *bars*, are not lacking. The spelling of proper names is just as great a problem; it is relatively easy to produce outrageous examples—*Cholmondeley* and *Marjoribanks* are familiar ones cited by Krapp (1925:169), and Scots *Auchinleck* and *Ruthven*, pronounced in ways that might be spelled *Affleck* and *Rivven*, are other favorites. In these respects, however, names do not differ from equally well-known common words like *boatswain*, *forecastle*, *woman* (from *wifmann*), *lord* (from *hlafweard*), or even *one*, whose initial /w/ is unexpected.

The unpredictable phonological development of such words and their often idiosyncratic spellings in present-day English are related phenomena, one being a consequence of the other. Such real or apparent exceptions can be found among both proper and common words, so Brøndal (1948:92) was indulging in hyperbole when he remarked that the pronunciation and spelling of personal names is "sans droit ni loi." Utley (1963:163), on the other hand, may have been too optimistic in his belief that "a whole new grammar of sound-change can develop from the close study of names and their startling variants," unless we are content with a historical grammar in which each word has its own history. The resistance of proper names to the historical changes that affect a language may have produced the situation in Finnish wherein proper names are exempt from synchronic phonological rules. Such a rough characterization is, however, no definition. Moreover, a phonologically defined class of names, if it occurs in any language at all, would certainly be an oddity of rare occurrence and language-specific.

Phonologically signaled proper names are either nonoccurring or extremely rare. Orthographically defined classes of words that correlate roughly with names as they are defined on other linguistic levels exist in some languages, including English. But English capitalized words are an autonomous class that have to be defined on the level of expression in orthographic terms; they reflect distinctions on other levels only fragmentarily and inconsistently.

3

Morphosyntactic Names

GRAMMARIANS have given a good deal of attention to the class of proper nouns defined in morphosyntactic terms. Syntactic criteria—that is, the item's relationships to other items in the same construction—have been most popular; but some attention has been given also to morphological criteria— that is, the relationships between the parts that make up the item itself when it is more than a single morpheme. The syntactic criteria most often cited are that proper nouns (1) are not used in the plural, (2) are not used with the range of articles available to common nouns, and (3) do not accept restrictive relative clauses as modifiers. The first criterion has been used by Jespersen (1924: 69), Bloomfield (1933:205), Sørensen (1958:156), Long (1961:39, 1969:109), and Strang (1968:114); the second by Jespersen (1909–49:7.437, 1924:69), Poutsma (1914:2.564), Kruisinga (1932:3.344), Bloomfield (1933:205), Christophersen (1939:79), McMillan (1949: 243), Gardiner (1954:21), Hockett (1958:311–13), Sørensen (1958: 156), Sledd (1959:244), Long (1961:39, 503, 1969:109), Chomsky (1965:100), Gleason (1965:134), Roberts (1967:17), Strang (1968:114), Zandvoort (1969:121), and Quirk et al. (1972:128, 160); and the third by Jespersen (1909–49:7.472), Sørensen (1958: 156), Utley (1963:173), Smith (1964:38), Long (1969:109), and Chafe (1970:292).

Any of the putative criteria taken alone is, however, inadequate for a satisfactory definition of proper names. Thus all of the following are possible:

I know a girl.

I know a Raquel.

All the girls I know are buxom.

All the Raquels I know are buxom.

20

A word like *Raquel* can be used in the singular or the plural, with *a* or *the*, and with or without restrictive modifiers. There are two probable senses of the word in such uses: 'person bearing the proper name in question' and 'person with some characteristics reminiscent of a known person bearing the name in question.' The second sense may seem less proper than the first; when, for a given name such as *quisling* or *martinet*, it ceases to be merely a nonce use and is conventionalized so that the name stands directly for the characteristic, 'traitorous puppet of foreign invaders' or 'strict disciplinarian,' rather than for the historical person, the name has clearly been commonized. There is, however, no clear reason to deny that the first sense is a proper use of the word. To anticipate chapter 6, if *Raquel* in "I know a Raquel" can be explained as 'a person with the name *Raquel*,' the name in "I know Raquel" can likewise be explained as 'the person with the name *Raquel*.'

The existence of the sentences cited above with the noun *Raquel* is an embarrassment for those who would maintain that proper nouns are used only in the singular and without articles or restrictive modifiers. Two approaches have been taken to explain away the offending sentences, both desperate measures. On the one hand, it has been proposed, in what may be called the Doppelgänger Effect, that *Raquel* in the sentence "I know Raquel" and *Raquel* in the expressions "a Raquel" or "all the Raquels I know" are really different, albeit homonymous, words, one a proper noun and the other a common noun (Bloomfield 1933:205; Strang 1968: 114; Chafe 1970:292; Hockett 1958:312 speaks of such names as having been "deproper-ized"). If this explanation is accepted, it follows that beside every proper noun in the language there is such a homonymous common noun. The consequence is unacceptable because it treats as an isolated, unpredictable lexical peculiarity what is really a general and completely predictable grammatical fact. Given any proper noun in English—from *Aaron* to *Zurich*—English speakers are free to talk about "an Aaron" and "the Zurichs that never were." Whatever can be accounted for by a general rule must be regarded as a grammatical fact, not a lexical accident (Bloomfield 1933:274). It is consequently a grammatical fact that all proper nouns can be used in the plural, with articles, and modified by restrictive clauses.

The other desperate solution, which might be called the Ostrich Caper, makes use of the Saussurian dichotomy between langue and parole to maintain that the use of *Raquel* in expressions like "a Raquel" and "all the Raquels I know" is an accident of the individual speech act and not a fact of the general language system (Gardiner 1954:12; Sampson 1970:131 is undecided whether the use is competent or only part of performance). But the uses under consideration are clearly a part of the English language because they are used by all native speakers and are not the result of this or that individual's caprice. To bury one's head in the langue will not suffice to make the offensive expressions disappear.

Although the criteria most often put forth as defining the grammatical class of proper nouns are inadequate, it is nonetheless true that there is such a class and that the commonly advanced criteria are based on correct, if insufficiently detailed, observations. Clarence Sloat (1969) has presented the most accurate characterization of the English proper noun, concerning which he observes that "the definite article will appear as zero before singular proper nouns, except when it is heavily stressed or they are preceded by restrictive adjectives or are followed by restrictive relative clauses." Sloat's observations need several qualifications, but they are basically correct.

Proper nouns may be indefinite, and when they are, they take the full range of limiting modifiers available to common unit nouns. (Whether proper nouns are ever mass nouns is a question that will be taken up later in this chapter; it is clear that most are unit nouns, and the question does not affect the argument.) Thus we have sentences like the following:

> I know a Raquel.
>
> I know some Raquels.
>
> I don't know any Raquels.
>
> I know every Raquel.

When a proper noun is definite, the article *the*, or one of the other definite determiners like *this* or *that*, is overtly present if the noun is plural:

> I know the Raquels.
>
> I know those Raquels.
>
> These Raquels are different from the others.

The article is also present if the definite proper noun is restricted:

I know the Raquel who has brown eyes.

I know the Raquel with brown eyes.

I know the brown-eyed Raquel.

Further, the article is present if it is the information focus (Halliday 1967–68:3.203) for the sentence and thus carries the sentence accent:

I know thé Raquel.

If, however, none of the four conditions obtain, so that the proper noun is singular, unrestricted, and definite without the definiteness being regarded as new information, the article cannot be present:

I know Raquel.

NOT *I know the Raquel.

Apart from this one relatively minor peculiarity, proper nouns are syntactically like other unit nouns:

COMMON	PROPER
A man is here.	A George is here.
Some men are here.	Some Georges are here.
The man is here.	ø George is here.
The man you know is here.	The George you know is here.
The men are here.	The Georges are here.

This one irregularity in the definiteness paradigm is, however, what defines the grammatical class of proper nouns. The three criteria noted earlier are thus correct, in that, with the added qualification concerning new information, their intersection is the irregularity that sets proper nouns apart from common ones.

There are a number of exceptions or apparent exceptions to the foregoing generalization. A large group of words like *Volkswagen*, *Spaniard*, and *Delicious* (apple) are regularly capitalized and therefore sometimes called proper, but they require *the* in circumstances that preclude the definite article for proper nouns: "The Spaniard in the Volkswagen wanted the Delicious rather than the

Winesap." These words offer no real problem. They are common nouns that, for a variety of reasons having nothing to do with grammar, are capitalized. They were discussed in chapter 2.

Words that are indeed proper names by the semantic criterion to be considered in chapter 6 include some that, like the preceding group, are syntactically common nouns and others whose syntax is that of proper nouns. These words fall into fairly clear subclasses that can be illustrated by the following names: *Vesuvius, Mount Olivet, Stone Mountain, the Mount of Olives, the Rocky Mountains,* and *the Matterhorn.*

Words like *Vesuvius* are straightforwardly names that are also proper nouns: *Bermuda, Kalamazoo, Broadway, Carl,* and *Thompson* are other examples. Words like *heaven, hell, purgatory, limbo,* and *paradise,* which are sometimes capitalized and sometimes not, are proper nouns in their syntax, but can be defined in a way other than the definition schema for proper names to be developed in chapter 6. Jespersen (1909–49:7.577) calls them quasi-proper names. There is also a group of nouns that are either proper or common, for example *parliament,* which is proper in "Parliament is meeting" but common in "The parliament is meeting." It is not clear that there is any semantic contrast between the two grammatical uses. Similar items are *congress, earth, scripture, god, teacher, cook, sister, father,* and other words of occupation and family relationship. Contrasting grammatical use of some of these words implies semantic differences, at least in the form of presuppositions. Thus "God will help" implies the speaker is a monotheist, whereas "The God will help" implies he is a polytheist. "Teacher will help" and "Sister will help" imply that the person referred to has the designated relationship to either the speaker or the one spoken to. The determiner-less noun may be understood as elliptical for either "my teacher" or "your teacher," but not usually for "his teacher." If A says to B about C, "Brother is here," an eavesdropper can confidently assume that C is brother to either (or both) A or B. If he is not, the appropriate form is "The brother is here," which has its own implication, namely that C is a brother to someone other than A or B.

Some words that are quite clearly semantic appellatives (as they will be defined in chapter 6) are grammatically proper nouns, for example *zero* as a point on the temperature scale (unlike *the freezing point,* which is semantically similar, although a common noun) and *sea level* as a point on the altitude scale (unlike *the fall line*). *First base* and other items of the kind have been mentioned in chapter 2. Another similar set (pointed out to me by James B. Mc-Millan) includes *librarian*, as in "John is (the) librarian at Chatta-hoochee," and so also *headmaster, dean, chairman, sheriff, janitor, purser, cashier, manager, conductor, pilot*, and a good many others, but not *stenographer, student, sophomore, plumber, dentist, cabbie, stewardess*, and so on. Those appellatives that can be used as grammatically proper nouns denote positions often involving some authority over others and, in grammatically proper use, denote one-of-a-kind positions within their hierarchies; such appellatives also have more frequent use as titles and are more often capitalized than the appellatives that are strictly common nouns in their grammar. To say "John is librarian" implies that he is either the only or the head librarian in a position of hierarchical responsibility. To say *"John is dentist" would be odd because dentists do not have a hierarchically defined position.

Not every use of a noun without *the* is proper use, however. To be proper, a noun must be regularly used without *the* under the appropriate circumstances. Thus, *the*-less uses of *school, college, prison, court, market, church, home, bed, breakfast, lunch, supper, automobile, plane, ship, train*, and so forth are not enough to make of those words proper nouns. When they are the objects of prepositions they may occur without *the*, as in "to school," "in bed," "at breakfast," "by automobile," and also in other uses in which they denote a kind of activity: "College is part of an education." In some such uses, the words are mass nouns, as can be seen from the mass-noun modifiers that occur with them: "enough school, too much school." In definite use as unit nouns, they require *the*: "He's going to the school."

Proper names of the type *Mount Olivet* or *Stone Mountain* consist of a general term and a specific, the order depending on what the general term is. Most general terms come second: *Yale University, Sherwood Forest, London Bridge, Biscayne Bay, Pennsylvania Avenue, Staten Island, Carson City, Niagara Falls, Carnegie Hall, Lincoln Center*, and *Penn Station*. The order general-specific occurs with fewer general terms: *Cape Hatteras, Fort Sumter*, and *Lake Leman* (compare the less common order for lake names in *Creve Coeur Lake*). Such composite names are similar to combinations like *chanteuse Hildegard, pianist Liberace, comedian Jack Benny, legislator Bella Abzug*; and these in turn blend into combinations of titles and names: *Senator Smith, Mayor Daley, Doctor Rubin,* and *Professor Hill.* Apart from the obvious semantic contrast of place versus personal names, the chief difference among these combinations is the extent to which the general term has been institutionalized as an accompaniment to the name.

In addition to the foregoing combinations of a general and a specific term by juxtaposition, many names are of the type *the Mount of Olives,* a noun phrase with the general term as head and the specific as the object of a modifying prepositional phrase: *the University of Wisconsin, the Forest of Arden, the Bridge of Sighs, the Bay of Biscay, the Avenue of the Americas, the Isle of Man, the City of Chicago, the Falls of the Rhine, the Cape of Good Hope, the Castle of Otranto, the Lake of Geneva,* and *the Sea of Japan.* Despite the semantic parallelism between names like *the Mount of Olives* and *Mount Olivet,* the former is grammatically common and the latter grammatically proper, since the first but not the second requires *the* under those circumstances in which it is required for common nouns.

Expressions of the type *the Rocky Mountains* are also examples of proper names that are grammatically common nouns. They too are very frequent: *the Great Plains, the Ozark Plateau, the Grand Canyon, the Bering Strait, the Persian Gulf, the Brooklyn Bridge, the Canal Zone, the Ivory Coast, the Orange Free State, the Soviet Union, the Black Forest, the China Sea, the Okefenokee Swamp, the Gobi Desert, the Pacific Ocean,* and *the Suez Canal.* The normal pattern is illustrated by *the Mississippi River,* in which the specific, *Mississippi,* serves as an adjunct within a noun phrase, *the river,* with the general term as head. More rarely the specific follows the general term, as in *the River Thames.* Among these constructions also, there is a lack of parallelism on the semantic and grammatical levels. *The Great Salt Lake* and *Lake Michigan* are names that are respectively common and proper nouns, whereas *the twelfth chapter* and *chapter twelve* are appellatives with the same grammatical difference between them.

Chapter twelve is an appellative because, as will be pointed out in chapter 6, its application is predictable in ways that the application of a name is not. A chapter that comes between chapters eleven and thirteen will necessarily be called *chapter twelve* by a general rule of numbering; there is no general rule to predict that the lake situated between Lakes Huron and Superior will be called *Lake Michigan*. *Chapter twelve*, however, is used without *the* under the same circumstances as *Lake Michigan*, and therefore both are grammatically proper nouns. The grammar of numbered items (as James B. McMillan has pointed out to me) is complex. An optional transformation might be postulated to relate surface common noun phrases like *the twelfth chapter* to surface proper noun phrases like *chapter twelve*, thus obliterating any distinction between them on a deeper level of analysis. But *the third anniversary* does not have a corresponding *anniversary three* in ordinary use, nor does *the eightieth highway* relate simply to *highway 80*. Moreover, with some nouns the ordinal form is syntactically proper: *Eighth Avenue*. Expressions such as *aisle two, precinct seven, (the) second grade, the third floor, uranium 235, P.S. 95, size twelve, vitamin A, section L, Mathematics 201*, and *grade B* or *B grade* (*movies*) present syntactic and semantic problems that await exploration but are beyond the scope of this study. Here it is enough to note that the members of pairs like *chapter twelve* and *the twelfth chapter* or like *Lake Michigan* and *the Great Salt Lake* differ in their surface grammar.

Another varied class of names are those like *the Matterhorn*, consisting of only a specific preceded by the definite article: *the Ukraine, the Transvaal, the Maghreb, the Negev, the Crimea, the Saar, the Tirol, the Congo, the Sudan, the Peloponnesus, the Hellespont, the Dardanelles, the Skaw, the Everglades, the Palisades, the Lido, the Alhambra, the Kaaba, the Kremlin, the Pentagon, the Alamo, the Escorial, the Vatican, the Hague, the Iliad, the Torah, the Koran, the Dhammapada, the Cid*. Despite the clear status of such terms as semantic names, the presence of *the* marks them as grammatically common. Whether a name requires *the* or does not is largely unpredictable. James Fenimore Cooper was apparently unable to decide whether the name of the title character of *The Deerslayer* was a characterizing epithet and thus a common noun that requires *the* or a genuine proper noun that rejects *the*. The last two references to the novel's hero are these: "Fifteen years had passed away ere it was in the power of the Deerslayer to revisit the Glimmerglass" and "The heart of Deerslayer beat quick as he found a ribbon of Judith's fluttering from a log." Although *Deerslayer* is as much a name in one use as another, its grammar fluctuates between that of common and proper nouns. Alternate names for the same referent and names for similar referents also show that it is highly variable whether such names are proper or common nouns. Thus *the Caucasus* is matched by *Caucasia, the Argentine* by *Argentina, the Netherlands* by *Holland, the Matterhorn* by *Vesuvius, the Bowery* by *Harlem,* and *the Bastille* by *Alcatraz.*

Some names of this sort have *the* idiomatically associated with them (*the Hague*) and have had it since their importation into English. Some have *the* as a result of ellipsis: *the Bodleian* (*Library*) and *the Metropolitan* (*Museum* or *Opera*). Perhaps ellipsis is also a reasonable explanation for the use of *the* with ship names like *the* (*ship*) *Mayflower, the* (*submarine*) *Nautilus,* and *the* (*carrier*) *Forrestal.* Others can hardly be explained as any kind of ellipsis but seem to result from a specialization of general terms: *the Piedmont, the Narrows, the Downs, the Weald, the Wolds, the Strand.* Such names are similar to the use of any general term with definite reference: *the Channel* (with reference to the English Channel regardless of what other channels may happen to be in the proximity of the speaker), *the City* (central London or New York), *the Coast* (California), *the Rock* (Gibraltar, Alcatraz, or even the Prudential Insurance Company), *the Lord, the Savior, the Father, the devil, the sun, the moon,* and *the Government.* It is difficult to distinguish the foregoing from any common noun used with *the* when the context makes the reference clear: "The president has nominated a replacement for the chief justice of the court"; "The president has appointed a replacement for the dean of the college." If the context is adequate to identify the referent, we talk about *the kitchen, the pool, the river, the capitol, the constitution, the lab, the chairman, the end zone,* and so on, like the Harvard secretary who is supposed to have informed a caller that the President was in Washington visiting Mr. Taft. Such expressions are common nouns in grammar and appellatives in meaning. The similarity between definite common nouns like *the queen* and names like *Elizabeth* has been noted (Christophersen 1939:70) but should not be exaggerated. The similarity lies in their mutual definiteness and thus equivalence of reference. It is a confusion of categories that makes for grammatical nonsense to say that *the queen,* with reference to Elizabeth II, is a name or a proper noun.

It is sometimes suggested that many of the above terms and others like *the universe, the creation,* and *the zodiac* constitute a special group of "uniques," appellative terms denoting a class of only one member (Christophersen 1939:24–25). Jespersen (1909–

49:7.482) has cogently criticized this view on the ground that in language there are no such classes. The fact that some words occur chiefly in the singular with *the* is an incidental consequence of the way the world is, not a significant generalization about language. *Equator* is used with the definite article *the* more than with the indefinite article *an* or with other determiners like *my* because there is, for each rotating body, just one equator; and by force of circumstance the earth is the rotating body whose equator is most often a topic of discourse. The fact that *the equator* is more common than *an equator* or *my equator* tells more about the world than about the linguistic system. It is therefore misleading to set up a class of "unique" nouns that generally occur in the singular with *the*.

It has also been proposed that the vocable *the* used with proper nouns like *the Hague* or *the Mississippi* is not the definite article, but something else: a part of the noun itself (Christophersen 1939: 61; Chomsky 1965:100; Roberts 1967:17; Strang 1968:114) or a meaningless noise (Sørensen 1958:156). Such interpretations are based on the assumption that names are not accompanied by determiners freely chosen from the definiteness system. It has already been argued that the assumption is mistaken. Proper names are generally used in the definite form, just as they are generally used in the singular and without modification, but they need not be so used. To say that *the* in *the Bronx* is something other than the definite article will entail that the category of definiteness, of which *the Bronx* is an exponent, is not explicitly realized in the name. This interpretation will make *the Bronx* and *Brooklyn* alike, in that neither uses the definite article to signal its definiteness, but the parallelism is achieved at the cost of a reductio ad absurdum: although *the Bronx* is definite, its *the* cannot be the definite article but must instead be an empty morph, definiteness having zero realization for all proper names. This triumph of rule over reality is similar to one structural explanation for irregular forms like *man/ men*, which held that the vowel difference is a nondistinctive consequence of a zero suffix on the second word. Instead of such occult explanations, we can say (1) for most nouns that are singular unrestricted names, the category of definiteness is unmarked; (2) for some, however, it is marked in the usual way, by *the*; (3) nouns with marked definiteness are "common," whereas those with unmarked definiteness are "proper."

The items so far discussed are only apparent exceptions to the definition of proper noun given earlier in this chapter. That they should ever have been thought exceptions is due to a confusion of categories from different linguistic levels, chiefly of proper nouns on the grammatical level with capitalized words on the orthographic level and names on the semantic level. Quite simply, *Vesuvius, Parliament, noon, zero, Mount Olivet,* and *Stone Mountain* are all proper nouns because they meet the definition of that grammatical class, whereas *the Volkswagen, the parliament, the afternoon, the freezing point, the Mount of Olives, the Rocky Mountains, the Matterhorn,* and *the sun* are all common nouns because they do not meet that definition. Perhaps the earliest grammatical treatment of proper nouns to recognize that cooccurrence with the definite article is the defining characteristic of the syntactic class and to accept the consequences of that recognition was James B. McMillan's study of place names (1949). If other grammarians had followed the consistency of his grammatical description, they could have avoided the dilemma that results from a monostratal view of language that assumes names and proper nouns must be isomorphic. There is not a perfect isomorphism between semantics and grammar. *Mount Olivet* and *the Mount of Olives* are both semantically names, just as *zero* and *the freezing point* are both semantically appellatives; but the first member of each pair is grammatically a proper noun and the second grammatically a common noun. Interlevel discrepancies of this kind are rife in language, but cannot be well understood without a view of linguistic structure that includes discrete levels.

There are, however, some genuine exceptions to the rule describing the use of *the* with proper nouns. First there is the use of the definite article with a Scottish family name to denote the head of the clan: *the MacNab, the MacGregor.* This semititle use is clearly marginal, for not only is it limited to the names of one ethnic group (*the Humplemeyer* and *the Jones* are nonoccurring), but most English speakers do not in fact use it at all. The historical status of the form is also marginal. The modern use seems to have been an innovation of Sir Walter Scott (Dallas 1913) popularized by his readers along with a number of words like *glamor,* which the *OED* says was extended to the literary language by his novels.

There is another use of *the* before personal names that is also marginal, although not so limited geographically or chronologically.

Christophersen (1939:114–15) cites Shakespeare, "My ancestor did from the streets of Rome the Tarquin drive"; Carlyle, "Stout Choiseul would discern in the Dubarry nothing but a wonderfully dizened Scarlet-woman"; the *Manchester Guardian,* "The real farmer's boy of these days is a smart lad with a motor-bicycle and views about the Dietrich and the Garbo"; and Dorothy Sayers, "There's the Meteyard. I must tell her what Armstrong said." The use, which seems faintly foreign and is reminiscent of French *la* as in *La Farge* or German *die* in reference to female artists and entertainers in the popular press, suggests preeminence of the person so distinguished, either in earnest or with a faintly mocking tone. This use is uncommon except perhaps in a somewhat old-fashioned expression like *the Magdalene,* which is analogous to *the Virgin.*

The two foregoing exceptional uses of *the* with proper nouns that normally reject the article are real exceptions to the general rule defining the grammatical class, but they are so limited in their scope that the generalization is not seriously affected by them. Another exception of a more serious nature pertains to the use of restrictive modifiers with *the*-less proper nouns. The exact nature of this exception depends on the kind of proper noun and on the kind of restrictive modifier it has. The pattern that we would expect is illustrated by the following paradigm:

NONRESTRICTIVE	RESTRICTIVE
George, who's governor	the George who's governor
George, from Alabama	the George from Alabama
conservative George	the conservative George

If a proper noun is modified by a nonrestrictive element, as in the first column, it is used without *the*; but if it is modified by a restrictive clause, phrase, or word, as in the second column, *the* is required. When the proper noun is a personal name and when the modifier is a clause or phrase, the pattern is followed fairly well. When, however, the modifier is an attributive adjective, two kinds of exception are common. First, a restrictive adjective may be used without *the*: "Are you voting for conservative George or liberal George?" Since the function of the adjectives in this sentence is to distinguish Georges, the adjectives are clearly restrictive. Second, a nonrestrictive adjective may be used with *the*: "the irrepressible Hubert." Because such a phrase can be freely used in a context involving only one Hubert, the adjective is clearly nonrestrictive. It would seem, then, that the generalization describing the use of *the* with proper nouns fails when the noun is modified by an attributive adjective.

There is, however, an important characteristic of restrictive adjectives modifying personal names that allows the generalization to be maintained in a slightly modified form. Consider the following sentences, in which clause accent is marked, thus indicating what is to be taken as "new information" in the sentence:

> The young Yeats was tálented, but the old Yeats was a génius.
>
> Yóung Yeats was talented, but óld Yeats was a genius.

Because clause accent is information-bearing, it is nonpredictable (Bolinger 1972); consequently other positions for the accent are possible in both sentences. Indeed, the two sentences can have exactly the same accent pattern—but not with the same effect. The accent positions indicated above are the normal, or unmarked, positions for the accent. Deviations from these positions imply special contrast, emphasis, or the like. Thus, when the information focus is on a part of the sentence other than the noun phrase, as in the first example, the restrictive meaning of the modifier is signaled by the presence of the article. When the information focus is on the restrictive adjective, however, the article can be omitted. Thus, to the definition of proper nouns must be added the provision that the definite article is also omitted optionally when the information focus falls on a restrictive attributive adjective.

Nonrestrictive modification with *the* like "the irrepressible Hubert" is a different problem. Such constructions are extremely common:

> the peripatetic Kissinger
>
> the admirable Crichton
>
> the Venerable Bede
>
> the Great Gatsby
>
> the Reverend Arthur Dimmesdale
>
> the Honorable Sam Massell

With these constructions it is instructive to compare postnominal modifiers of the type "Alfred the Great," "Ethelred the Unready," "Ivan the Terrible," and noun appositives like "Priestley the chemist," "the chemist Priestley"; "Mary the Virgin," "the Virgin Mary." Common noun phrases that include the definite article can occur either before or after a proper noun to which they are appositive. Postnominal adjectives preceded by *the*, such as "Alfred the Great" or "Hubert the irrepressible," are best accounted for as headless noun phrases: "Alfred the Great (one)," "Hubert the irrepressible (one)," thus making them parallel to noun appositives and suggesting the proportion:

Priestley the chemist: the chemist Priestley::

Hubert the irrepressible: the irrepressible Hubert.

Given the foregoing proportion, we can say that just as "Hubert, who is irrepressible" can be paraphrased as "irrepressible Hubert," so "Hubert, who is the irrepressible (one)" can be paraphrased as either "Hubert, the irrepressible" or "the irrepressible Hubert." Under this interpretation, constructions like "the irrepressible Hubert," "the peripatetic Kissinger," and "the Venerable Bede" do not violate the generalization that nouns modified nonrestrictively omit *the*, because the article accompanies the adjective rather than the noun, giving the constituent structure ((the irrepressible) Hubert) as opposed to the constituent structure of noun phrases with restrictive adjectives: (the (conservative) George).

Thus far only proper nouns that are personal names have been considered. Other kinds of proper nouns, such as place names, offer somewhat different complications. Like personal names, place names modified by a restrictive clause require *the*: "the America that the colonists knew." Unlike personal names, however, place names have *the* optionally when they are modified by restrictive phrases: "(the) America of the colonial period"; and when the restrictive modifier is an adjective, *the* is usually impossible or unlikely: "ancient Greece," "eastern Europe," "outer Mongolia," "cisalpine Gaul," "residential Chicago," "theatrical New York," "coastal America," "contemporary London." Some adjectives can be used either with or without *the*, although with some probability of a contrast of meaning: Thus, "the old Atlanta" and "the new Israel" may suggest a chronological dimension, 'the Atlanta of yesteryear'

and 'the Israel of today,' whereas "old Atlanta" and "new Israel"
may imply chiefly a geographical dimension: 'the old part of Atlanta' and 'the occupied territories of Israel.' Which adjectival
modifiers of place names resist *the* and which permit it with what
distinctions of meaning are questions still to be answered, and
whose answers will require that a large corpus of data be surveyed.

Similar problems regarding restrictive modifiers, especially adjectives, arise with other kinds of proper nouns. For example, holi-
day names, for which *the* seems to be optional when a restrictive
adjective is present: "Hanukkah is (the) Jewish Christmas, and
Easter is (the) Christian Passover." In general, the use of *the* with
restrictive adjectives remains to be fully explained.

Proper nouns can be characterized by their cooccurrence with
the definite article, although the rule must be qualified, as has been
pointed out, when restrictive phrases or adjectives are present. A
number of other syntactic peculiarities have also been suggested
for proper nouns, none of which are reliable as definitions. It has
been observed, for example, that proper nouns do not freely accept
adjective modifiers (Long 1961:39; Strang 1968:114). While it is
undoubtedly true that adjectives occur more often with common
nouns than they do with proper nouns, such a statistical generalization seems to be a consequence of the way proper nouns are used,
a matter of pragmatics, rather than an insight into the syntactic
nature of the word class. Adjectives do occur with proper nouns.
Although a relative clause, as in "They will nominate Teddy, who
is charismatic" is more to be expected than an attributive adjective,
as in "They will nominate charismatic Teddy," the latter is never-
theless grammatical. Moreover, familiar expressions like "wily Ulys-
ses" and "merry old England" are normal enough, and new epithetic
combinations are readily accepted, such as "spunky George Wallace," which became commonplace in the news media shortly after
the assassination attempt. If there are limitations on the use of adjectives with proper nouns, they seem to be matters of frequency
or to depend on the lexical items involved—and thus to be of only
limited interest to a grammarian.

Jespersen (1909–49:7.458) has proposed that proper nouns are
never used as predicate complements, a view shared by Lyons
(1966:213). In this idea Jespersen was consistently applying two
other proposals of his, namely that subjects are always more specific
than their predicate complements and that proper nouns are the

most specific of all words, from the conjunction of which it follows that proper nouns cannot be predicate complements. The conclusion can be maintained in the face of sentences like "the author of this book was Otto Jespersen" only by the device of saying that in such cases the proper noun is really the subject and the apparent subject is really the predicate complement (Jespersen 1924:153). The claim is thus vacuous, for counterexamples are simply reinterpreted in conformity with the original claim. Jespersen's view of proper nouns as the most specialized of all words, coupled with his opinion that modifiers must be less specialized than the words they modify, also led him to the conclusion that proper nouns are never modifiers (Jespersen 1924:77). This conclusion is equally vacuous, since Jespersen would account for exceptions like *a Pinter play* by maintaining that in this use *Pinter* is not a proper noun.

Archibald A. Hill (1958:232), on the contrary, recognizes that a proper noun can be used to modify a noun in immediately prenominal position, as in "the good old Smith house," a position shared by common nouns: "the good old stone house." Hill says that common nouns can also occur as modifiers in predicate position: "The good old house is stone"; whereas proper nouns cannot: *"The good old house is Smith," in which construction a genitive is instead required: "The good old house is Smith's." This distribution is, as Utley (1963:172–73) notes, a genuine characteristic of adjunct use; it is not, however, a unique characteristic of the adjunct use of proper nouns. When the proper noun has a different sort of referent, for example "the good old Miami house," neither paraphrase is possible: *"The good old house is Miami" nor *"The good old house is Miami's." Instead, what is required is "The good old house is in Miami." Similarly, for "the beach house," the acceptable paraphrase is "the house is on the beach," the difference in preposition being attributable to the complex, but for the present purpose irrelevant, system of locative expressions in English. So too, for "the blacksmith shop," the paraphrase is "The shop is the blacksmith's." The form of the predicate expression is determined not by whether the noun modifier is proper or common but by whether its referent is a person like *Smith* or *blacksmith*, a place like *Miami* or *beach*, or a material like *stone*. The attributive position of such modifiers disguises differences that appear in the predicate position. If English were more Germanish, it might be possible to talk about *"the good old in-Miami house," thus preserving the distinction.

Dwight Bolinger (1971:61–66) has pointed out a way in which proper nouns are like unmodified definite common nouns. He observes that certain kinds of adverbial modifiers can come between the verb and its object only if the object is a modified noun phrase: "They took with them the youngest boys" is acceptable, but *"They took with them the boys" is not, or at least is less so. The same distinction is found with proper nouns: *"They took with them John" is unacceptable, whereas "They took with them the youngest John" is permissible. To the extent that proper nouns share such restrictions with common nouns, they are seen to be essentially the same sorts of words, with only the special restriction on the occurrence of the definite article to distinguish them.

Some recent generative grammars have distinguished proper from common nouns by introducing a binary feature such as COMMON (Jacobs and Rosenbaum 1968:60; Stockwell et al. 1968:982), PROPER (McCawley 1968:134), or UNIQUE (Chafe 1970:112) in the lexical entry of every noun, so that *boy* might be marked + COMMON, whereas *Bill* would be marked – COMMON. The danger in such a purely taxonomic feature is that it may be mistaken for an explanation. It is what Lakoff (1971:ii) has called fudge: "A fudge, as any student of the physical sciences can tell you, is a factor that you add to what you've got to give you what you want to get. . . . One of the principal ways of fudging is to give a phenomenon a name rather than to provide an adequate description of it." A feature like PROPER explains nothing. At best it is a flag marking a part of the grammar that needs attention; at worst it disguises the need for description. It is still necessary to discover whether each word is common or proper, to specify the criteria by which the discovery is made, and to decide what effect the difference has. Generative grammar has so far provided no such insight into the nature of proper names.

It has been proposed that generic nouns are in some respects like proper names (Christophersen 1939:59; Hill 1966). While it is possible to suggest somewhat vaguely that they are "proper names for a whole class," there is no significant formal parallelism. The generic use of a noun, as the chart below shows, can be indefinite singular or plural, definite singular, or unspecified singular. What may be thought of as the typical case is a unit noun like *horse*. *Man* is an exceptional unit noun, in that it lacks the definite generic ("The man is a biped" can only refer to some specific man),

INDEFINITE SINGULAR	INDEFINITE PLURAL
A horse is a quadruped.	Horses are quadrupeds.
A man is a biped.	Men are bipeds.
A Datsun is a compact.	Datsuns are compacts.
Milk is a liquid.	———
A Sue is a female.	Sues are females.

DEFINITE SINGULAR	UNSPECIFIED SINGULAR
The horse is a quadruped.	———
———	Man is a biped.
The Datsun is a compact.	Datsun is a compact.
———	———
———	———

having instead a form that is unspecified for the category of definiteness. *Datsun* and other names for products have the full range of possibilities. Mass nouns like *milk* have only a single generic form: they lack number contrast in any use and are without a definite generic form. Proper nouns like *Sue* also have only indefinite generics, a peculiarity they share with some common nouns for which a definite generic would be odd—plural nouns like *trousers* and abstract nouns like *thought* and *estimation*.

It is perhaps worth noting, as already observed by Long (1961: 236), that citation forms are syntactically proper nouns. "*Horse* has five letters" is syntactically like "Harry has five senses," and "The *accommodations* on this page are all misspelled" is like "The Algernons in this room are all misguided." The syntactic parallelism is, of course, not matched by the semantics of the expressions, although it may suggest that citations are something like "proper names" for the utterance type of which they are citations.

It is also noteworthy that the proper/common distinction is neutralized when a noun is used in the vocative function, as in "Listen, Aristotle" versus "Listen, man." Any noun in vocative use is necessarily definite; the person addressed may be assumed to know his own name and to know which appellatives are applicable to him.

Because indefinite reference is not a possibility under these circumstances, the formal contrast between it and definiteness is not made at all. The result is that all vocatives appear to be proper nouns; but since there is no contrast between the two word classes in this function, it is preferable to say that the distinction is neutralized.

It is often assumed that the distinction between unit and mass is not relevant to the class of proper nouns, usually because the latter are thought to represent a prior subcategorization (all nouns are either proper or common; all common nouns are either unit or mass). Most proper nouns are indeed unit nouns, but there is at least one group of words in which the categories of mass and proper seem to intersect. Mass nouns are those that (1) have no plural, (2) have a simple indefinite form without *a*, and (3) are modified by words like *much, little, less,* and *a lot of* rather than *many, few, fewer, each,* and *every*; thus: *fun, much fun,* not **a fun, *many funs.*

Names of languages have the foregoing characteristics. They resist plural formation: **Frenches*; reject the indefinite article: **a Spanish*; and accept mass modifiers: "much English, little Latin, less Greek, and a lot of Arabic." Language names can depart from these characteristics, for example in referring to Great Russian and White Russian, one might speak of "the two Russians," and it is possible to distinguish between "a prestigious Italian" and "an Italian of the streets." But all mass nouns can be used in those ways, as "a malicious fun" and "a fun that is innocent" are "two different funs." There is no reason to deny that language names are mass nouns. On the other hand, they have also the principal characteristics of proper nouns. They require the definite article when they are modified by a restrictive clause: "the Hebrew that I know," but not when they are unrestricted: "I know Hebrew."

Thus it appears that the proper/common system and the unit/ mass system are overlapping categories for which nouns must be independently specified. Although proper mass nouns are limited in range, they do exist. Long (1969:112) noted that language names belong to the class of mass nouns, but he drew from that fact the conclusion that therefore they are not true proper nouns. Long's conclusion seems to rest on his initial, traditional but unwarranted, assumption that mass and proper are mutually exclusive categories.

Names of illnesses such as *tuberculosis, appendicitis, influenza, arthritis,* and *indigestion* are possibly another group of proper mass nouns. They are clearly mass nouns: all resist the plural and the indefinite article. Because of the nature of the illnesses, degree modifiers are semantically odd with some of them in some uses (witness the strangeness of saying that someone has "a lot of appendicitis" although it is not strange to say that there is "a lot of appendicitis among the students" and it is normal to say that someone has "a lot of indigestion"). It might be doubted that such words should be called proper, but they generally reject the definite article except when they are restrictively modified: "He has influenza and arthritis," whereas other disease names do not: "He has the flu and the gout." Still other disease names are not only common, but also unit nouns: "a cold," "a plague." The fact that words belong to the same semantic set is no guarantee that they will belong to the same grammatical classes. The use of articles with disease terms is too complex for an easy generalization about their grammatical class.

Although the syntax of names has been most thoroughly studied, their morphology has also been given some attention (Long 1969), particularly the morphology of special kinds of names, such as those for store-front churches (Dillard 1968) or place names (McMillan 1949; Zinkin 1969). It is impossible, however, to say anything positive about the internal grammar of names that is true of all, for different kinds of names have altogether different internal structures. The analysis of English personal names into given name, first name, middle name, family name, maiden name, married name, generational tag, and so forth—or of Icelandic names into given name and patronym or of Roman names into praenomen, nomen, and cognomen—has no application to names of places or of other things.

It is not even the case that names have to be morphological nouns or noun phrases, an assumption sometimes explicitly (Sørensen 1958:156) or implicitly made, but easily falsifiable. Hockett (1958: 311) cites Menomini personal names like [ana·ma·nahkwat] 'under a cloud' and [awa·nohape·w] 'he sits in a fog' as instances of proper names that have internal structures alien to the noun class. Lévi-Strauss (1966:177) points out that one of the standard name patterns among the Iroquois consists of a verb with an incorporated noun: *He-raises-the-sky, He-announces-victory, She-works-in-the-house.* It is not necessary to have recourse to the exotica of Amerindian tongues for such examples. The names of "convenience" stores in any American town, for example *U-Pak-Em,* will show nonnominal internal grammar, as do the *U-Haul* and *U-Drive-It* companies. The *Dare to Be Great* organization was in the news recently under charges of fraud, presumably for daring too much, and the *I Can't Believe It's a Girdle* girdle has been widely touted on television. The names of racehorses are an unfailing source of native exotica: *More, Sincere, Unintentionally, Communicate, In Focus, Little But Fast, Who's Afraid, Hurry Up Dear*, and *Gee Judge* have been reported by Long (1969:109, 120); racing forms will furnish a good many others. Although such names have regular nominal syntax, their morphology is exceedingly diverse.

Personal names are sometimes nonnominal in their etymology and also in their synchronic grammar as far as they are subject to internal analysis. Thus prepositional phrases underlie *Attebury* 'at the borough,' *Atwood*, and *Atwell*; and verbal or adjectival expressions are behind *Golightly, Dolittle, Fullalove, Lovejoy, Makepeace, Turnbull* (Matthews 1966). The latter group of names reminds us that not only names but appellatives also are not necessarily nouns in their internal grammar, witness *scarecrow, pickpocket*, and *spoilsport*, whose simplest derivation traces them to verb phrases. It is easy to exaggerate the oddity of exotic languages. During the sixteenth and seventeenth centuries, the Puritan population of England produced some fruity specimens (Bowman 1931:91), given names like *The Lord Is Near, From Above*, or the justly famous *Praise-God Barebones* and his even more memorably named brother *If-Christ-Had-Not-Died-For-You-You-Had-Been-Damned Barebones*, known to his familiars as *Damned Barebones*. Other worthies of the period were *Faint-Not Dighurst, Be-Steadfast Elyarde*, and the doubtless sincerely named *Flie-Fornication*, the bastard son of Catrus Andrews. *Accepted Frewen*, archbishop of York, and his brother *Thankful* are evidence that even the establishment shared the vogue for giving characterizing names not limited to nominal morphology.

It has been repeatedly demonstrated in this chapter that the grammatical distinction between proper and common nouns is not isomorphic with the semantic distinction between names and nonnames. Words that belong to the same semantic set are treated syntactically in different ways. *The Great Salt Lake, the Everglades, the Bastille, the Cid*, and *the Bronx* are grammatically common nouns, whereas *Lake Erie, Yosemite, Alcatraz, Charlemagne*, and *Brooklyn* are grammatically proper. Yet all are names.

On the other hand, baseball terms like *first, second*, and *third base* illustrate a discrepancy of a different sort in that semantically they are not proper names but ordinary appellatives like *outfield, dugout,* and *mound.* But whereas the latter are common nouns, requiring an article, as in "He went from the outfield to the dugout and then to the mound," the former are proper nouns used, when singular and unrestricted, without the definite article: "He is on first base."

It is also obvious that grammatically defined proper nouns are language-specific. Some other languages have distinctions like that of English. Thus Hockett (1958:311–12) reports that in Fijian a particle *ko* marks proper nouns in contrast to the particle *na,* used with common nouns, so that *na vanua levu* means 'the big island,' whereas *ko vanua levu* means 'Big Island.' Other languages, however, such as Latin, in which *via longa* can be either 'the long road' or 'Long Road,' have no particles by which to distinguish proper from common nouns and thus may not have the distinction as a syntactic category at all.

Of those items that are generally recognized as proper names, some have the internal structure typical of nouns, others do not; some have an incompatibility with the definite article that marks proper nouns, others are common nouns. These facts make it impossible to treat names as a simple grammatical class. It is necessary to distinguish between names defined morphosyntactically—proper nouns—and names defined in some other way (Sledd 1959: 244; Long 1961:503, 1969:107). The question that remains to be answered is in what other way names can be defined.

4

Referential Names

THE EARLIEST and far and away the most often used definition of proper names describes them as words used to refer to single, particular, or unique individuals—names for classes that have only one member. This definition, which seems to have originated among the Stoics, appears in the oldest of Western grammars, that of Dionysius Thrax, and was popularized in Europe by the *Ars Minor* of Donatus. Thus Dionysius says that a proper noun is one which signifies an individual or particular substance (idian ousian), whereas a common noun signifies general substance (koinen ousian); and Donatus's catechistical grammar runs thus: "Qualitas nominum in quo est? Bipertita est: aut enim unius nomen est et proprium dicitur, aut multorum et appellativum." Here we have the two dominant themes of this definition: a proper name applies to a single individual (unius nomen est) that is a particular, unique being (idia ousia). The themes can be seen again in the definitions of the seventeenth- and eighteenth-century writers of universal grammars, such as the Port Royal grammar (Lancelot 1660:29), which distinguishes between proper names as expressions for single things and appellatives as expressions for several similar things, or James Harris's *Hermes* (1751:345), which holds that proper names are expressions for particulars as opposed to general ideas.

More recently, a similar approach has been taken by many grammarians, of whom the following are representative: Jespersen (1922:438) speaks of "proper names of the good old kind, borne by and denoting only one single individual," thus suggesting that we must deal also with a bad new kind of name that is not so restricted. Bloomfield (1933:205) defines the class meaning of proper names as "species of object *containing only one specimen* [Bloomfield's italics]." Collinson (1937:21) believes that "a proper name refers to a particular individual and to no other." So also, "A proper name is a symbol directly identifying a single individual" (Christophersen 1939:62), and "A proper name, in so far as it remains a real proper name, is a word which refers only to one individual thing, usually a person or place" (Gardiner 1951:41). Gardiner later retracted this definition (1954:22), but it continued to be held by Coseriu (1967:279): "*El nombre proprio* . . . es siempre nombre de un 'singular,'" and by Palmer and Blandford (1969:45). Emphasis has been placed on the referential uniqueness of proper names by Brown (1851:239), Curme (1935:1), Long (1969:109), Chafe (1970:112), Stageberg (1971:283), and Quirk et al. (1972: 160), to mention some grammatical treatments of different kinds and purposes.

A definition honored by such long and persistent use and exemplifying such uncommon accord between the ancients and the moderns should carry great weight. Yet quite apart from the philosophical problem posed by the notion of a unique individual, which was acknowledged by Jespersen (1924:69), the definition does not define the class of items it is intended for. Although all languages certainly have means of referring to particular, single individuals, it is not clear that, of those words we might want to call proper names in natural human language, any uniquely refer to particular, single individuals. On the contrary most of them clearly do not (Hockett 1958:312).

Words like *Andes* and *Antilles* that are plural in form are no particular problem. They have no singular *Ande* and *Antille* and therefore may be taken as applying globally to that which they designate (Jespersen 1924:64). They are not essentially different in this respect from collectives like *Mafia*, which though formally singular can take either singular or plural concord; the grammatical number of a noun is largely an arbitrary way of interpreting the number of things. Gardiner (1954:24) believed that words like *the Medes* and *the Angles* were a more serious and indeed an insuperable problem, because they have singulars, *a Mede, an Angle*. If such words are proper names, Gardiner was correct; they seem, however, to belong with *Ford* and *Volkswagen* as appellatives, except when used as names of the tribe, not tribal members.

Nor is it of any linguistic consequence that there are proper names to which no actual persons or things correspond, names like *Xanadu, Pegasus, Mary Poppins,* and *Smaug.* Such words pose a philosophical problem that has been resolved in various ways, including the paradox of Russell's view (1905:479) that "a phrase may be denoting, and yet not denote anything," or his other view (1940:37) that if the thing a "true proper name" purports to name does not occur, the name is meaningless. For linguistics, however, the problem does not exist, for the grammarian is not concerned with the ontology of linguistic referents. For him it is enough to know whether a speaker intends that two terms shall have the same or different referents; whether those referents are of this nature or of that is a problem that the grammarian is happy to leave to the philosopher. With the new-found respectability of mentalism in linguistics, some linguists no longer share Mill's conviction (1843: 1.2.1) that "names are names of things, not of our ideas," and talk rather about "items in the speaker's mental picture of the universe" in distinction to "real things in the universe" (McCawley 1968:138), but that may be more a convenience than an ontological commitment. For the linguist, *Xanadu* has as good a referent as *Canada,* and in neither case does it make any difference to him what sort of referent it is.

A more serious problem is that most personal names and many place names are in fact applied to any number of different persons and places (Strawson 1950:188; Long 1961:229). There is many a Tom, Dick, or Harry in this world. There are more Athenses than the one in Attica, and more Cairos than the one in Egypt. As Leonard Linsky (1963:76) has paronomastically observed, "Proper names are usually (rather) common names." It is possible, to be sure, to point to an occasional proper name that seems to have a unique referent—*Popocatepetl* is one—but there is nothing to stop Congress tomorrow from deciding to rename Pike's Peak *Popocatepetl,* thus destroying the uniqueness of reference. When a proper name refers to a single individual, it seems to be an accident of use, a fact of parole, and not a matter of the language system. There is nothing in English or apparently in any other natural language that requires a name to have unique reference.

In view of the obvious fact that most personal names and many place names have more than one referent associated with them, the position that proper names have unique reference can be maintained only by recourse to the notions of homonymy or polysemy. That is, we can say either that *John* as applied to John Adams and *John* as applied to John Baker are different words that happen to be pronounced alike or that they are the same word with different meanings. Two items with the same pronunciation but different meanings may be said to be the same polysemous lexical item if they have the same grammatical distribution, that is, if they belong to the same part of speech and follow the same rules of syntactic concord. Otherwise, if the meanings are correlated with some grammatical distinction, the items must be accounted different, although homonymous, words. For example, *iris* belongs to the same part of speech and in other respects is grammatically unchanged regardless of whether it is taken in the sense 'flowering plant' or the sense 'part of the eye.' It is therefore polysemous—one word with several senses. *Pupil* 'student' and *pupil* 'part of the eye,' on the other hand, are two homonymous words because the former requires personal and animate gender concord (*who, he* or *she*) whereas the latter requires impersonal and neuter concord (*which, it*). Etymology, the touchstone most often used by dictionaries in deciding whether two items are the same or different words, is irrelevant to the synchronic question.

The distinction between polysemy and homonymy is, however, a Tweedledee-Tweedledum one for the problem of *John* as applied to John Adams and John Baker. Both approaches maintain that a vocable like *John* has a different sense as it is applied to different referents. This view in one form or the other has been suggested by such contemporaries as Gardiner (1954:16), Hockett (1958: 312), Sørensen (1963:83–86), and Chafe (1970:112, 274).

The view, however, has some consequences that are unacceptable either theoretically or practically. If we say that homonymy is involved, we will be forced to conclude that there are as many different words *John* as there are or have been or will be persons bearing the name. As the person John^x differs from the person John^y, we shall have to say that the name *John* applied to the first is a different word from the name *John* applied to the second. This position makes the vocabulary infinite and thus in principle indescribable. Genuine cases of homonymy, like that of *pupil*, involve two or three or some relatively small number of distinct words that are pronounced alike. They do not involve an infinite number of different words. Polysemy is no better as an explanation, for by it we must say that the word *John* has as many meanings as there are, were, or will be persons so named. The vocabulary is still unlimited and indescribable because every proper name has a potentially infinite number of meanings. It is as though we should say that *iris* has not just a few senses, including the two mentioned above, but as many senses as there are individual flowers of the family Iridaceae. The consequence would be to make definition impossible. In either of these approaches, meaning is confused with reference, since there is assumed to be a one-to-one relationship between meanings and referents. The distinction between that which a word means and that to which it can be used to refer is an important one that has been painstakingly made by students of language such as Frege (1892) more recently and in the thirteenth century by Peter of Spain (Mullally 1945:3–5). It should not be lightly abandoned, and certainly not for the sake of maintaining an otherwise faulty definition. The notions of homonymy and polysemy, as they have been applied in onomastics, provide no tools for handling the data of proper names; on the contrary, they make description impossible. Instead of explaining the use of proper names, they avoid explanation by confusing meaning and reference—a confusion that would not be permitted for appellatives.

It would appear that the traditional view of proper names as words for unique individuals cannot be maintained, or can be maintained only at a very high cost—that of increasing the size of the vocabulary beyond all manageability. But if that is right, we might wonder how it is that the traditional view has been held so long and by so many. There are two main reasons. First, what traditionalists said was in many cases not what they meant. The plain sense of the traditional definition is that a proper name is a term for one and only one particular referent. What seems rather to have been meant is that within any given discourse, the speaker may use a name with the intention of identifying a particular individual and that he further assumes the person spoken to will succeed in identifying that individual from the name. This is quite a different thing from saying that each name of itself has unique reference, independent of its verbal and situational context. What those who have spoken of a unique referent seem often to have intended is the grammatical category of definiteness.

It has been proposed that proper names are inherently definite (Jespersen 1924:65; Bloomfield 1933:205; Sørensen 1963:92; Postal 1966:204; Chafe 1970:198), just as personal pronouns, demonstratives, and adverbs like *here, there, now,* and *then* are inherently definite (Leech 1969:277). But this proposal rests on the unstated assumption that words are proper names only if they have definite reference, and is thus really a definition in disguise. If proper names are defined in some independent way and then it proves to be the case that they are always definite, an insight into language structure has been gained. That, however, is not the case. When we consider paradigmatic cases of the proper name—words like *George, Jones, Moscow*, and *Siam*—it is clear that they are usually, but not invariably, definite (Langendoen 1970:124), because of expressions like "a George" and "any Moscow."

It might be said that for many names, definite reference is the unmarked state, whereas for most appellatives, indefinite reference is the unmarked state. Such a conclusion is supported by the formal syntactic signals of English grammar. Thus when appellatives occur without determiners, for example the mass noun *water* in "He drinks water" or the plural unit noun *men* in "They employ men," the reference is indefinite, whereas a determiner-less name like *Bill* in "They employ Bill" is definite in its reference. This formal distinction in modern English parallels what seems to be a widespread feeling about the difference between proper names and appellatives even in those languages like Greek or Latin which lack such formal signals. If this markedness relation is correct, it explains both why grammarians since the Stoics have thought that proper names denoted unique individuals (that is, had definite reference) and why the formal signals of modern English should have developed as they did. It can perhaps be accepted as a general principle of historical change that a language tends rather to develop overt markings that reflect covert categories than to lose them or to develop overt markings at variance with covert categories. A characteristic distinction between proper names and appellatives is that we expect the former to be definite and the latter indefinite rather than the other way around. *Bill, water*, and *men* are simpler not only in form but also in meaning than *a Bill, the water*, and *the men*.

That names are not invariably definite can, however, be seen in a language like Armenian, in which a name such as *Arto* may occur either with or without the definite article (Der-Houssikian 1970: 8–9). Thus in the sentence *Arton egav* 'Arto came' the name requires the suffixed definite article *-n* in normal circumstances, in which the speaker assumes that the addressee knows the identity of the referent. If the situation is such that the addressee cannot be assumed to know the identity of the referent, for example in "I have a friend called Arto," the article is not used. Expressions of the type "named, called X" that include a citation of the name are linguistically special in some ways to be described in chapter 6, but it is worth noting here that also in English such expressions are basically indefinite, alternating, as they do, with an overtly signaled indefinite form of the name: "Someone called George is here to see you" and "A George is here to see you" are equivalent expressions with respect to indefiniteness.

It is not the case, however, that all proper names use an unmarked form for definite reference. *The Alamo, the Appalachian Mountains,* and *the Lake of Geneva* are proper names whose definiteness has to be marked. In an attempt to save definiteness as a defining criterion for proper names, Waismann (1965:196) has proposed that names are single words rather than "syntactically formed groups of words," thus excluding an expression like *the murderer of Caesar* as a proper name while allowing *Brutus.* This distinction would, however, exclude also *the Lake of Geneva,* as clearly a group of words with a syntactic structure, *the Appalachian Mountains, Lake Leman, Mount Pisgah, the Alamo,* and quite likely *Marcus Junius Brutus* as well. Such paradoxes can be avoided by recognizing units on more than one linguistic level. Semantically, all of the items cited in the last sentence are proper names. Those that take *the* are common nouns or noun phrases; those that do not are proper nouns or noun phrases. Definiteness is then a category shared by names and appellatives. Many names are like *Lake Leman* in being morphologically unmarked for definiteness; others are like *the Lake of Geneva* in being marked for the category. The categories PROPER and DEFINITE are not equivalent. Reinterpreting the traditional view of the uniqueness of proper names as a matter of definite reference will not account adequately for the diversity of use of such names in ordinary language.

The second reason that the traditional view has held sway is that it has confused ordinary language with the specialized register used in logical discourse. As already noted, the earliest grammatical speculations of the Hellenic world did not distinguish purely linguistic description from philosophical considerations. Grammarians are still to some extent influenced by the categories of logic, especially in dealing with names.

The logician finds it necessary to have some way of identifying what are, within his universe of discourse, unique referents. He consequently specifies such ways and often calls what is so defined a proper name, although such "proper names" coincide very imperfectly with the class of items that the grammarian might want to designate. Frege (1892:57), for example, defined *proper name* as a sign for a definite object, thus embracing both *Brutus* and *the murderer of Caesar* within the class. Russell has said a great many, not always consistent, things about names; but for him *this* is as good a proper name as *Homer*, indeed rather a better one (Russell 1919:179; 1940:116–37), and a name is an indivisible symbol "whose meaning is something that can only occur as subject, *i.e.* ... an 'individual' or a 'particular.'" The latter view has been taken up by a number of grammarians (Jespersen 1909–49:7.458; 1924: 153; Lyons 1966:213). Although it may be true by definition for "logical" languages, it is false for ordinary language on two counts: proper names do not always name particulars since they occur grammatically indefinite, and particular terms are not limited to the subject function of ordinary linguistic structures.

Russell (1905; 1919:179) and Quine (1950:220–24) developed a method of eliminating singular terms, that is, logically proper names, from logical discourse by the expedient of making predicates out of them. Thus *Homer* may be expressed something like "There is a y such that for every x, x is-Homer (Homerizes) if and only if x is y." A somewhat similar use of variables has been proposed for natural languages (Bach 1968:110–11). Although the idea that the deep structure of human speech is the predicate calculus may seem not far removed from Householder's (1971:xi) tongue-in-cheek proposal that the fundamental form of a language is Morse code, more will be said about it in chapter 6.

Linguists have often benefitted from the work of philosophers, who see the subject matter with which both are concerned from a different and potentially fresh point of view; however, it is not clear that the philosophical concern with particulars has any relevance to natural language. The linguist Charles Hockett (1958: 312) has cogently remarked that "to logicians, a 'proper name' or 'proper noun' is a symbol which designates an entity of which there is only one. . . . In actual languages there are no forms which can be so described, save possibly through pure accident." And a logician concerned with ordinary language, Leonard Linsky (1963: 76), has also recognized that proper names need not involve a unique relationship between the name and the one named: "What is indeed necessary, if I am to make a definite assertion, is not that one person only be named 'Tommy Jones,' but that I be referring to just one person, however many others there may be with the same name as his." For the description of natural languages, as opposed to purely logical systems, we must add that for definiteness, it is necessary not only that the speaker be referring to just one person, but also that he have reason to believe that, within the context of the language act, the person addressed will be able to identify the one intended. If the speaker is referring to a specific person but has no reason to think the addressee can make a correct identification from the name, he refers not to "Tommy Jones" but rather to "a Tommy Jones" or the like. Definiteness reflects the speaker's assumptions about the knowledge of those he speaks to and about the situation in which the name is used.

In a contrast of proper names with common appellatives, there is often a confusion between the linguistic system and the use of that system. Thus Gilbert Ryle (1957:139) believes "it is obvious that the vast majority of words are unlike the words 'Fido' and 'London' in . . . that they are general. 'Fido' stands for a particular dog, but the noun 'dog' covers this dog Fido, and all other dogs past, present, and future, dogs in novels, dogs in dog breeders' plans for the future, and so on indefinitely." What Ryle believes to be obvious is instead a muddle of two different aspects of language. *Dog* covers all the dogs Ryle indicates—living and dead, actual and projected, real and fictional—as an item in the lexicon, a linguistic abstraction. *Fido* stands for a particular dog only in some particular context, as when a woman says to her husband, "You'd better take Fido for his walk." In such a context, however, *dog* is just as particular as *Fido*. Thus the woman might have said instead, "You'd better take the dog for his walk," without intending all those dogs whose specters Ryle invokes. Conversely, *Fido*, considered abstractly, as a characteristic name for a dog, is a general term too. Admittedly it is not so general as *dog*, but that is because Fidos are a proper subset of dogs, just like terriers or one-eyed, tailless hunting dogs.

The use of a word like *dog* or *Fido* in some particular context should not be confused with the word as an abstraction, a lexical unit available for use when it is needed. To compare *dog* as an isolated lexical unit with *Fido* in a particular contextualized use is to compare incommensurables and reveals nothing about the differences between the two words.

The contrast drawn here between the linguistic system considered in the abstract and a particular application of the system reflects in part the Saussurian distinction between langue and parole and in part the logicians' distinction between the mention of a form and its use. Gardiner (1954:8–10) draws the same contrast when he distinguishes between "disembodied" and "embodied" proper names, which are, respectively, names considered in isolation and names taken in some context. It is likewise reflected in the familiar distinction between MEANING and REFERRING, used by philosophers and grammarians alike since Peter of Spain (Pope John XXI) drew the distinction and called it SIGNIFICATION versus SUPPOSITION. A linguistic form has reference to some thing or state of affairs only when it is used in a particular context, whereas it has meaning even in isolation, merely by virtue of its being a linguistic form. If a word's meaning is the set of conditions under which it can be used appropriately, its reference is what, in some particular use, it is being used for.

Two tokens (*Fido* as uttered by one person and *Fido* as uttered by another or by the same person a second time) count as the same use of the type (the lexical form *Fido*) provided they have the same reference, and as different uses otherwise. There is thus a three-way distinction between a type (which is a matter of the language system), the use of a type (which is a way the system can be applied), and the utterance of a type (a token, a speech act). As Strawson (1950:171) observes, we cannot say the same things about these three. Those who contrast the "uniqueness" of proper names with the nonuniqueness of common appellatives are generally contrasting a use of the former with the latter as a type. Nothing whatever is thereby shown about the forms, for uniqueness is a characteristic not of the meaning of types, but of a particular referential use. In this respect names do not differ from appellatives, which also have unique uses, as in "this dog," "my father," or "a certain book," provided these phrases are considered in contexts in which they have genuine use and are not merely mentioned, as in this sentence.

"Disembodied" proper names considered in isolation are, as Gardiner observed (1954:8), the subject of linguistic studies concerning their etymology, their frequency of occurrence, and other intralanguage facts. "Embodied" proper names, as they are used in context, are treated in encyclopedias, biographical dictionaries, gazetteers, and so forth, where the subject of interest is not the word itself, but the things named by it. The distinction between lexical and encyclopedic facts, which has been dealt with by Gove (1965), is not always easy to make, but it is of both theoretical and practical importance, especially to onomastics, for any effort to define a proper name by its referents is to move out of language into other areas of study.

Language has reference, and some linguistic expressions (singular terms) are used to refer to single unique individuals: *George Washington Carver, my eldest child, the tallest living woman, the car, he*, whereas other expressions (general terms) do not purport to be so specific in their reference: *most scientists, a girl, any house, someone*. This difference in reference is, however, clearly not coterminous with the distinction between names and appellatives.

5

Semantic Names: The Degree of Meaning

LOSELY associated with the view that proper names have singular reference is the view popularized by John Stuart Mill that names are words without signification, meaningless marks by which one thing is distinguished from another. Thus, *boy* has a meaning, something like 'nonadult male human being,' and refers to various creatures, whereas *Bill* has no meaning, but merely refers to some creature. In Mill's terminology (1843: 1.2.5), a proper name is nonconnotative, that is, it identifies an individual without imputing any attributes to him. According to Mill, Cratylus was wrong, for Hermogenes could bear one name as well as any other, all being equally meaningless.

Mill's view has been held also by Christophersen (1939:59), who says that names lack any conceptual content and thus indicate an object without implying a description of it; by Strawson (1950: 188), who holds that names have neither descriptive meaning like common appellatives nor general rules like pronouns and demonstratives, but are governed by ad hoc conventions that have to be established for each application of the name to a different person; and by Togeby (1951:215), who would have names stand for individuals rather than semantic classes; and also by others who phrase the matter in still other ways but whose views are essentially those of Mill. It is customary to speak of this definition of the proper name as Mill's, and certainly it is he who is chiefly responsible for its modern use; however, its substance can be found in earlier authors, such as John of Salisbury's "Nominantur singularia sed universalia significantur" (cited by Jakobson 1972:78)—Individual things are named, but general classes are signified.

Some who have shared Mill's view of names as nonsignificant have rephrased the distinction between them and appellatives as one of intensional versus extensional classes (Johnson 1921:94). A class

53

that is defined by specifying some attribute or combination of attributes shared by all and only the members of that class is intensional, for example, a class consisting of all men who are over six and a half feet in height, are bald, and have an even number of fingers on their left hands. The membership of such a class may be unknown; indeed it may have no members at all. But because the defining attributes are clear, if anyone with those attributes exists he will belong to the class. On the other hand, a class that is defined simply by listing its members is extensional, for example, a class consisting of Swami Vivekananda, strawberry jello, and the first sentence of Jane Austen's *Pride and Prejudice*. The membership of this class is known, though it is doubtful that there is any attribute in common to the three members. Intensional classes are defined by specifying general characteristics, extensional classes by listing membership. An appellative like *boy* would label an intensional class, of which the defining attributes are 'human, male, nonadult.' A proper name like *Bill*, however, would label an extensional class, which has no defining characteristics—no connotative meaning—but whose membership can only be listed: Bill Bailey, Bill Buckley, Bill Hitchcock, and so on.

For Mill, proper and common names are alike in denoting things but differ in that common names, in addition to denoting, imply attributes. For others (Austin 1961:7; Sørensen 1963:14), the two kinds of words differ in that, whereas proper names denote without connoting, appellatives connote without denoting directly. This extension of Mill's view makes proper names a thing apart from other nominal terms in language. It makes of them, in fact, something very much like the variables x, y, z of mathematics and logic. Proper names have been likened explicitly to such indexical symbols (Hockett 1958:312; McCawley 1968:138); and Sampson (1970: 103–4) has proposed that names do not belong in the lexicon of a language at all, but rather in a separate component, the "topicon," whose function is to account for referential identity and difference within a discourse. Treating proper names as not part of the lexicon avoids one problem that otherwise arises: if all names are equally meaningless, then every name is presumably a synonym of every other. This conclusion has been accepted by Togeby (1951) but is surely a reductio ad absurdum. The fact that substituting one name for another within a sentence can radically alter the meaning of the sentence and its truth value suggests that names must have nonsynonymous meanings. If names are not part of the lexicon, as Sampson would have it, we cannot expect them to be subject to categories like synonymy any more than x, y, or z.

There are other problems with Mill's view that cannot be so easily disposed of. According to his definition, the application of any name to an individual is purely arbitrary, being quite independent of any characteristic of the person, and thus one name is as appropriate as another. For some linguists, the arbitrary imposition of a name is the decisive criterion by which the class can be defined: "Entscheidendes Kriterium eines Namens ist, dass er willkürlich gewählt bzw. gegeben wird" (Witkowski 1964:50). In one sense, most words, or more precisely morphemes, are arbitrary, in that they are noniconic, the exception being onomatopoeic terms, although even words like *crash, moo,* and *hiccup* are conventional since there is no necessary relationship between their sounds and meanings. The arbitrariness that is imputed to proper names is, however, of a different sort. If a speaker of English acquires as a pet a domesticated animal that chases mice and purrs, his decision to refer to it as *a cat* is not arbitrary, but reflects his knowledge of the English language; on the other hand, his decision to call it *Miko* may be wholly arbitrary. Thus, the arbitrariness of proper names applies to their initial bestowal on an object.

Yet there are several respects in which not all names are arbitrary. Many speakers would consider it odd to name a cat *Fido* or *Rover*. Gilbert Ryle (1957:137) agrees with Mill in supposing "from the fact yonder dog is Fido, no other truth about him follows at all. No information is provided for anything to follow from. Using a proper name is not committing oneself to any further assertions whatsoever." But Ryle's example, in fact, suggests a different conclusion from the one he draws. The fact that yonder entity is Fido may not have any necessary logical implications, but the ordinary use of the name *Fido* in ordinary language certainly presupposes that the entity so named is a dog, and not a cat or a boy. Any other use of the name would be odd. A few years ago, a song entitled "A Boy Named Sue" was popularized by Johnny Cash; its lyrics describe the hard but educative life led by a boy whose father had nothing to give him but a name that would ensure he would learn to defend himself. If names were really arbitrary, the song would have no point. McCawley's (1968:139) argument that "Gwendolyn hurt himself" is odd in the same way as "My neighbor hurt himself," when the latter is said of a woman, ignores the fact that the first is odd in isolation, without reference to any context whatever, and the second is not.

To be sure, not all given names are distinctive in gender. Some are sexually ambiguous: *Evelyn, Beverly, Tracy, Robin,* and *Dana,* for example (Prenner 1942). In the South, hypocoristic forms of male names, such as *Tommie, Jimmy,* and *Johnnie,* are usual for females, although often in parataxis with more conventionally female names: *Tommie-Sue, Johnnie-May.* Imaginatively invented names and the use of family names (often the mother's maiden name) as first names for both males and females further blur the distinction between the gender of given names. The distinction, however, exists, as demonstrated by the fact that exceptions to it are causes for comment. Names like *Sue,* and *Fido* as well, do have meaning and imply something about the ones named.

Family names present a different kind of nonarbitrariness. To say that a name like *Miller* or *Smith* is arbitrarily given (Christopher-sen 1939:60; Witkowski 1964:49–50) is misleading, and an argument to the effect that persons called *Miller* or *Smith* need not be millers or smiths is merely a red herring. Whatever the provenience of the name, no ordinary user of the language supposes that a man called *Miller* grinds grain for a living, but ordinary users do suppose, with considerable justification, that Mr. Miller's father was also called *Miller,* and likewise his brothers, his unmarried sisters, his wife, and his children. Family names are not, as a rule, arbitrarily given to an individual, nor are they capriciously changed, although they may be for due cause and with respect for appropriate procedures (Smith 1969; Ashley 1971).

There have been occasions, even in recent history, when such arbitrariness was characteristic of family names, for example among the black population of the South in the immediately postbellum years. Former slaves, in assimilating to the structure of white society, arbitrarily took family names and often new first ones as well; more-over, they changed those names at will, so that a freedman might take on and put off a variety of names or even bear several simul-taneously. "For instance, a boy entered school under the name of Joseph Marshall; the boys called him Marshall Black; and the name given him by his parents, and by which he was called at home, was Joseph Black Thomas" (Donald 1952:151). Each member of the family might have a different last name. If such an arrangement were the normal one for "family" names, they could be said to be arbitrary. That arrangement, however, was clearly not normal, but rather a transitional one in which members of the population that had formerly had no family name system were acquiring one; in the process they treated "family" names like given names, which need not be shared by members of a family unit, and both like nicknames, which can be freely changed at the whim of the name-users.

Nicknames, although in one respect at the opposite pole from family names in that they are neither customarily passed on to progeny nor stable during an individual's lifetime, are also usually nonarbitrary, albeit in a different way. Minnesota Fats was not so nicknamed arbitrarily. If he had been called instead *Slim*, the naming principle (lucus a non lucendo) would have been different but not the nonarbitrariness of the name. Some bynames may be arbitrary, but they are not the typical sort; indeed, the usual function of the nickname is to suggest some characteristic of the person named, that is, to be nonarbitrary.

There are many peoples among whom the formal given name cannot be arbitrary; personal names, for example, may be required to contain a reference to the clan's totem. Thus typical names for members of the Black Bear clan of the Osage tribe are *Flashing-eyes*, *Tracks-on-the-prairie*, *Black-bear-woman*, or *Fat-on-the-skin*; names with allusions to another clan's totem would be impossible (Lévi-Strauss 1966:173–76). Also nonarbitrary are the day-names mentioned in chapter 1 and ordinal names with the sense 'first born' and the like (Lévi-Strauss 1966:189–90). Even in American naming practices, some families have a tradition of giving the eldest son the name of his paternal grandfather; such "grandfather names" may be bestowed with a regularity that is beyond arbitrariness.

An important and much studied sort of nonarbitrary proper name is the characterizing name (also known as label name, attributive name, or charactonym) used in literary works. Examples in the English tradition are as old as *Unferth* (that is, 'Marpeace') of the *Beowulf* epic and as recent as *J. Alfred Prufrock, Frodo*, or *Alexander Portnoy*, with such intervening notables as Chaucer's Man of Law's *Constance, Falstaff, Lady Wishfort, Mrs. Malaprop, Pippa, Arthur Dimmesdale*, and numerous others. Such names have been treated by Robinson (1972) and Green (1972), and in the 1968 issue of *Names* (vol. 16, no. 4) devoted to literary onomastics.

To turn from personal to place names, it is sometimes suggested that names like *Mont Blanc, Dartmouth,* and *Land's End* are impure proper names because their parts are meaningful and appropriate, and thus they are not wholly arbitrary (Gardiner 1954:42; Shwayder 1963:56). These words indeed exemplify another kind of non-arbitrariness in names. The particular problem they raise is not limited to onomastics, however, for it does not differ essentially from the semantic problem posed by any idiom—an expression with meaningful parts whose total meaning cannot be predicted from the meanings of those parts—for example, nominal expressions like *bluebird, scarecrow, bull's eye,* verbal combinations like *look out, come around, call on the carpet,* or even whole clauses like *A rolling stone gathers no moss.* All idioms, including proper names of the kind mentioned, pose an interesting problem in the relationship of the lexicon to the grammar, but it is not a specifically onomastic problem.

The notion that, because proper names are arbitrary, expressions like *Mont Blanc, Sue,* or *Slim* are names to a lesser degree or not names at all is, as Utley (1963:151) observed, "a kind of categorical obsession," completely at variance with ordinary language. To take words like *Vercingetorix* or *Popocatepetl* as better examples of proper names than *Sue* and *Dartmouth* because the former are arbitrary, at least to most English speakers, whereas the latter have some descriptive value, is to ignore the obvious fact that most names have some motivation. Those that do not are the exception, not the paradigmatic case. Indeed, the notion that any name is arbitrary and unmotivated is a relatively recent one. As Elsdon Smith (1966:492) has pointed out, "In the past people simply did not confer names from sheer whim and without any meaning. It would be contrary to man's nature to name the objects of his thoughts by sounds which conveyed no meaning to him or others." There are, to be sure, names that spring from whim—the pungent examples collected by Thomas Pyles (1947, 1959) are good illustrations: *Glathu, Aletrice, Juhree, Naul, Twyla, Zazzelle, Onan, Phalla,* and *Merdine,* which one hopes were unmotivated on the part of the parental name-givers. Still, this kind of naming seems to be an aberration. The fact that names are keys to the past for the historian and the philologist is evidence that they are more than meaningless index symbols.

It has also been maintained by Bertrand Russell (1940:116–37) and Hockett (1958:312) that proper names are like substitutes, such as personal or demonstrative pronouns, in serving a deictic rather than a descriptive function, since they are supposed to point out rather than characterize their referents. Although there is some, albeit unclear, likeness between proper names and pronouns, there are important differences. Russell himself has observed that "the word 'men' is applicable to all the objects called severally 'a man,' but the word 'these' is not applicable to all the objects severally called 'this' on different occasions." In this respect, proper names are more like appellatives than like pronouns; for when pluralized (*Cairos, Georges, Joneses*), they are applicable to all the objects severally called by the singular name (*Cairo, George, Jones*). Just as "The man is mortal" is implied by "All men are mortal," so "George is intelligent" is implied by "All Georges are intelligent." "This is good," on the other hand, is not implied by "These are good," unless we have knowledge derived from some other source that the "this" of the first sentence is one of the "these" of the second sentence. Such independent knowledge about the referents is not required for appellatives or for proper names.

In support of the proposition that names have no meaning, it has been averred that they are not translated (Vendler 1967:38; Mańczak 1968a:206; Zabeeh 1968:69). But it is by no means clear that the assertion is correct. On the contrary, names of different languages correspond in three ways that can be called translation.

First there is the treatment of names like *Krasnaya Ploshchad*, the name of an architectural feature in Moscow, which is rendered into English as a calque, *Red Square*. This is translation of a name in the most obvious and least interesting sense. It is essentially the same thing we do when we say that *Mont Blanc* means 'white mountain,' *Peter* means 'a rock,' and *Emanuel* means 'God with us,' although in these cases the etymological calque is not used as a name. In the case of *Red Square* or *Hall of Supreme Harmony* (T'ai-ho-tien) or the *Yellow River* (Huang Ho), it is hard to see how one can avoid saying that the name has been translated. Indeed, the names of one class, the titles of books, songs, paintings, and so forth, are regularly so translated.

The second kind of correspondence that can be called translation is illustrated by English *John*, Spanish *Juan*, Russian *Ivan*, Italian *Giovanni*, German *Johannes*, Scots Gaelic *Ian*, and so forth. The fact that such names are parallel historical developments of a common prototype is not crucial, but the fact that they are used in parallel ways and serve as equivalents, for example in biblical translation, is decisive. Place names of the type are *Vienna* and *Wien, Florence* and *Firenze.* Items that have no etymological connection but which are functionally equivalent in the same way are *Finland* and *Suomi, Germany* and *Deutschland, Everest* and *Chomolungma.* To say that the first word in each set is the English version and not the English translation of the others is to quibble over terminology (in that we might as well say that *dog* is the English equivalent rather than translation of *Hund*) or to argue in a circle (if we assume names cannot be translated, then names that are apparently translational equivalents must be something else). Although equivalences of this kind are different from calques, in which idiom formation is involved, both can reasonably be called translation.

The most common sort of equivalence, however, is one that has seldom if ever been thought of as translation, but which has a good claim to the title. When we use one language, such as English, and wish to refer by name to a person, place, or other nameable thing from a culture in which another language is used, and if there is no readily available calque or equivalent of the kinds noted above, the usual procedure is to find out the name in the native language and then to render it in some approximate way in English. Such rendering takes place in either of two forms. Suppose the foreign name is Spanish *Quixote* [kixóte]. On the one hand, we may imitate the foreign pronunciation in some reasonably close way, allowing for differences between what sounds are found in each language phonemically and phonetically and for phonotactic differences between the two languages. Thus the Spanish name may be rendered into English [kiyhówdi]. The first two vowels, simple in Spanish, are diphthongized; the last vowel, being unstressed, has to be replaced by a different one in the English dialect considered here, which permits final unstressed [i] but not [e]. The second consonant, a velar fricative in Spanish, is replaced by its nearest English equivalent, aspiration. The last consonant, a Spanish dental, is replaced by an English alveolar and further is voiced, since this variety of English pronounces *latter* like *ladder, atom* like *Adam,* and so in all similar environments. The process just described is familiar to linguists under the term "sound substitution."

Alternatively, the spelling of the foreign name may be adapted to English. In the case of *Quixote,* the Spanish spelling and its

English adaptation are identical; however, if the foreign language uses a nonroman alphabet or a nonalphabetical writing system, such as the Cyrillic alphabet or the kana syllabaries, the written form will require change. In either case the spelling is then pronounced in English according to the rules of English orthoepy. The name *Quixote* so treated yields the pronunciation [kwíksət] or [kwíksòt]. This is the familiar process of giving a spelling pronunciation to the transliteration of a foreign name.

Sound substitution is the phonological equivalent and transliteration is the orthographic equivalent of translation. As translation is the pairing of lexical and grammatical units in two languages, so sound substitution is the pairing of phonological units and transliteration the pairing of orthographic units. In themselves they are not translation but devices by which a language borrows words, whether names or other sorts of words, from a foreign tongue. Once such a word has been borrowed, it becomes a part of the borrowing language in phonology, morphology, and syntax, although it may for some time continue to be marked as a "loan word" or "foreign vocabulary" in a variety of ways. As part of the borrowing language, it is available to serve as a translation of the corresponding word, its etymon, in the native language. We do not usually say that English *Quixote*, however pronounced, is a translation of Spanish *Quixote*, but there is good reason for doing just that. The English name can be regarded as a translation of the Spanish because the two have parallel uses, for instance when the former serves as a translational equivalent for the latter in reference to the fictional character from La Mancha. (On the similar but more specific question of the naturalization of immigrants' surnames, see Dykema 1972.)

The process just described whereby a name is borrowed, and thereafter is available to serve as a translation of its etymon, is not different from the same process applied to common words. Thus the American soldier stationed in Japan acquires the Japanese word for 'good-bye' by sound substitution as [sàyənádə], and the student of Indian religion acquires a Sanskrit philosophical term as *dharma* [dármə] by transliteration and spelling pronunciation. Thereafter either term is available as an English translation for the foreign equivalents. The loan word *dharma* is favored as a translation of the Sanskrit technical term because possible calques, such as *law*, fail to cover adequately the semantic area of the Sanskrit word. The popular loan *sayonada* is a close equivalent to the older English *good-bye* except in associations and circumstances of use; it, however, is also an English word because it is used in English contexts and conforms to all the rules of English. As such, it is available for use as a translation of the Japanese word transliterated *sayonara,* although the availability of the better established and nearly synonymous *good-bye* may preempt it.

Dharma* and *sayonada* are both recent loans, and the latter may well not survive the generation among whom it originated, yet their process of borrowing is not significantly different from that which resulted in *street* or *wine* or *episcopal* at an earlier time. Nor is the process that has resulted in any of those words significantly different from the one that introduces proper names like *Quixote* into English. The subsequent use of all such loan words as equivalents for their etyma must be called translation, unless an arbitrary and a priori terminological distinction is to be made. Consequently the proposition that names are not translated cannot be used in support of their meaninglessness.

To regard proper names as words with no linguistic meaning but only extralinguistic reference suggests that they are not really part of language. There are those who have maintained that names are indeed not a part of language (Harris 1751:346; Strawson 1950:186; Vendler 1967:38; McCawley 1968:138–39), but the idea is counter-intuititive and smacks of the old dodge whereby the only language facts that are recognized are those that can be conveniently handled by the available theory. Utley's (1963:165) view that "a grammar which does not include proper names is no grammar at all" has more to recommend it.

Sometimes instead of holding that names themselves are not part of language (which seems transparently false), the position is taken that knowledge of names is not part of knowledge of a language. So put, there is a sense in which the view is correct. A speaker of English may never have encountered the name *Blavatsky* or, having encountered it, may not know that it is applied to such and such a person. He would not thereby cease to be a speaker of English, and in that way it can be said that knowledge of names is not knowledge of the language. However, what has just been said about names is also true of appellatives. A speaker of English may never have encountered the word *blastophore* or, having encountered it, may not know it applies to such and such a thing. He would not cease to be a speaker of English for that reason either. Complete knowledge of the vocabulary available to English speakers is not a prerequisite to being an English speaker. It would certainly be unusual if a speaker did not know the words *blame* or *blanket* or *blast*, but it would also be unusual if he did not know *Boston* or *Blondie* or *Black Forest*. The lack of such knowledge would be debilitating in the easy use of English but would not prevent it altogether. Paraphrases of various sorts could replace each of the individual words. On the other hand, if a person knew no common nouns at all or were unable to use common nouns appropriately in sentences, it would certainly be said that he was not really a speaker of English; and substantially the same thing could be said about a person that knew no proper names or was unable to use any members of the class in appropriate ways. Ignorance of either class as a whole would be radical ignorance of the language system.

To say that ignorance of names, unlike ignorance of appellatives, is not ignorance of the language may imply something like the following: X, who is a speaker of English, encounters Y on the street while both are watching a building under construction. They have a short conversation about the construction, the weather, and team-standings in the National League. Then they part without having introduced themselves. X does not know Y's name. Yet X is not ignorant of the language. But then neither is he ignorant of names; rather he is ignorant about Y, a nonlinguistic matter. If this is what is intended, the catchphrase has been wrongly put and should rather be "Ignorance of a person is not ignorance of a language," which is true enough but is not a statement about names. In no sense is it true that there is some special way in which names can be considered not part of language.

The assumption that names are words with reference but no meaning can lead to a number of corollaries: that they are like variable indices or pronouns, that they are applied arbitrarily, that they are untranslatable, and that they are not part of a language at all. These corollaries have unacceptable consequences in ordinary language, and so Mill's view must be rejected as inadequate for linguistic ends.

In a position that seems to be directly opposite Mill's, Sweet (1891:1.59), Bréal (1897:183), and Jespersen (1922:438, 1924:65–66, 71) have argued that since proper names are more specific in reference than common nouns, they must connote more attributes and be therefore the most meaningful of all words. The fewer things a word stands for, the more specialized it is and the fuller its definition must be in order to circumscribe the few objects, or in the case of proper names "of the good old kind" the single object, of reference. The views of Mill and of Sweet and the others are, however, not so much opposites as different statements of the same position that seem contrary because they use the same words, *meaning* or *connotation,* in different ways. Thus, Mill and Jespersen both talk about connotation but understand it differently. Mill intended a minimal set of defining characteristics, whereas Jespersen seems to have had in mind the totality of a word's associations. If we take Frege's (1892:56) three-way distinction between referent (the thing to which a sign refers), sense (the conditions under which a sign may appropriately refer to a thing), and association (ideas arising in a speaker's mind from memories of sense impressions), for Mill *connotation* was 'sense' and for Jespersen 'association,' a variation in use of the term that still exists. This is not to suggest, however, that Jespersen and the others were unaware of the distinction; Jespersen was familiar with it but denied that any sharp line can be drawn between the essential characteristics (sense) of a word and the accidental ones (association).

Because Jespersen did not distinguish between a word's basic sense and its associations, the question of how it is that proper names like *Quisling, Silhouette, Moll, Macintosh,* or *China* become common appellatives seemed to him to be a crucial one. He thought that in making them common words, we focus on one part of their meaning—which requires that they should have more meaning as proper names than as appellatives. The question is certainly important, as is also the opposite one of how common appellatives like *charity, red, smith,* or *long island* come to be used as proper names, and how they differ from the pseudo-proper use of words like *Father, Mother,* and *Teacher.* But it is not clear that any of these questions have the importance for the definition of *name* that Jespersen assumed. Semantic change is not limited to narrowing and widening the scope of a word's meaning; *buxom* did not acquire the sense 'busty' nor *tiger* the sense 'aggressively virile male' through generalization or specialization, but rather through a process of transfer that involves the associations of the words. There is no problem when a proper name like *Martinet* is taken to mean something associated with one of the persons who has borne it and thereby becomes an appellative, nor need such change of meaning imply that the name *Martinet* is more meaningful than the appellative *martinet*.

One of the problems with the Sweet-Jespersen view is that it makes proper names impossible to define in the way appellatives are, that is, by specifying those characteristics of things by virtue of which they can be referred to by the word. It would be necessary, in effect, to give a complete description of the thing, a practical impossibility with odd consequences (Searle 1958:169). Worse, however, is the fact that this approach, like that of Mill, identifies the meaning of a proper name with the thing or things it refers to. Mill makes the identification openly by allowing proper names no connotation but only denotation; Sweet and Jespersen make it covertly by equating the meaning of a name like *Plato* with the totality of characteristics by which the person Plato is distinguished from all other persons. In both cases the meaning of a word has been made coterminous with a particular thing, and thus, as suggested in the last chapter, linguistic and nonlinguistic facts are confused.

A third position, and a tertium quid between that of Mill and that of Sweet and Jespersen, is the one proposed by Frege, in which it is supposed, as in the others, that proper names refer to single unique objects but in which it is held, with Sweet and against Mill, that names have connotative meaning. The problem implicit in Sweet's view, that the sense of a name threatens to become infinite by embracing every fact by which the person named is different from every other person, is avoided through the expedient of supposing that the sense of the name is limited to some manageable set of facts that may differ for every user of the name:

> In the case of an actual proper name such as 'Aristotle' opinions as to the sense may differ. It might, for instance, be taken to be the following: the pupil of Plato and teacher of Alexander the Great. Anybody who does this will attach another sense to the sentence 'Aristotle was born in Stagira' than will a man who takes as the sense of the name: the teacher of Alexander the Great who was born in Stagira. So long as the reference remains the same, such variations of sense may be tolerated, although they are to be avoided in the theoretical structure of a demonstrative science and ought not to occur in a perfect language. (Frege 1892:57–58)

Frege's view is echoed in Russell's (1905, 1918) proposal to re-place the proper names of ordinary language with descriptions: "When we ask whether Homer existed, we are using the word 'Homer' as an abbreviated description: we may replace it by (say) 'the author of the *Iliad* and the *Odyssey*'" (Russell 1919:179). The view has been argued also by Searle (1958, 1969) and by Sørensen (1963).

One of the problems with the intermediate view is that the mean-ing of a name is made a wholly private matter. Each name can and probably does have a different meaning for every person who uses it; there is no public definition for any name. Moreover, there is a different set of such unlimitedly numerous private meanings for every person or thing to which a name is attached. Furthermore, for any speaker who knows two names for the same individual, such as *Cicero* and *Tully* or *Stalin* and *Dzugashvili*, those names would ap-parently be synonyms, thus making statements of the form "Dzu-gashvili was Stalin" analytically true for that speaker, a position accepted by Searle (1958). Similarly, Frege was apparently willing to accept as a consequence that the statement "Aristotle was born in Stagira" would be analytically true for anyone who takes as the definition of *Aristotle* 'teacher of Alexander the Great who was born in Stagira' but not for one who takes as its definition 'pupil of Plato and teacher of Alexander.' These are odd consequences.

John Searle (1958), in supporting Frege's view, has argued that using a name to refer to an object presupposes the truth of a set of uniquely referring descriptive statements that are regarded by users of the name as essential and established facts about the object. It is the nature of this set of statements, however, that it should be open, since what is regarded as basic established fact about an individual is subject to easy revision; it is at any given time unspecified, and if we should be required to specify the set, the decision as to what facts belong to it would have to be made arbi-trarily. Searle seems prepared to accept these consequences, but for the grammarian they vitiate any usefulness in the proposal. A meaning that consists of an indefinite, unknown, and arbitrary set of statements is no meaning worth bothering with, for it cannot be defined and is beyond agreement or disagreement. Furthermore, if the sense of a proper name were always an imprecise one (Searle 1969:140), then we should be in doubt about how to apply the name. But that is not the case.

In addition to its own special difficulties, this view of the meaning of names shares with those of Mill and Sweet a confusion of langue and parole, of the system of language with its application. Consider two putative definitions of the expression *my son*: (1) 'first-degree male descendent of the speaker' and (2) 'twelve-year-old (in 1972) residing with the author of this study.' The former is a possible definition for linguistic study in that it is applicable to any correct, literal use of the expression. The latter is not a definition at all, but a characterization of one possible referent of the expression. The former, an intensional definition, is a statement about the expression's meaning in the English language; the latter, an extensional definition, is a description of one of the objects of which the expression might be used. The Mill-Sweet-Frege approach to defining proper names deals exclusively with extensional definitions. That approach is doubtless useful for logic but has no application whatever to the meaning of names in a linguistic sense, because extensional definitions are about things rather than about language.

The problem of defining proper names is intransigent enough to have led Jespersen (1924:70–71) to the conclusion "that no sharp line can be drawn between proper and common names, the difference being one of degree rather than of kind," a view shared by Bréal (1897:182–83), Pulgram (1954), and Mańczak (1968a: 218). But such a throwing up of hands is unsatisfactory, if for no other reason, because it means that onomastics would be without a clearly definable object of study—a consequence not dear to the heart of onomatologists. But more important, the conclusion is unsatisfactory because ordinary language implies, and twenty-four hundred years of scholarship has assumed, that all languages have names that are somehow clearly different from other sorts of words. A theory of names that fails either to take account of those facts or to define its object satisfactorily is inadequate.

6

Semantic Names: The Kind of Meaning

F THE amount of meaning a name has, whether none or infinite or some unspecified intermediate quantity, is not an adequate characterization of the class, the kind of meaning may be distinctive. It will be helpful, therefore, to look at some of the ways a name can be used to see whether there is a clue in them to a more adequate definition of the term. In each of the following sentences, *Thomas* is used in a different sense:

1. His name is Thomas.
2. Here are Catherine and Thomas.
3. She was a Thomas before she married.
4. I remember a younger Thomas.
5. He is trying to be another Thomas.
6. Looking in the mirror, he saw a Thomas looking back.
7. The dress she bought is a genuine Thomas.

In the first sentence, *Thomas* is really a citation form and might more properly have been written in italics: "His name is *Thomas*." The sentence in which it occurs is a metalinguistic one, being language about language. Such uses must be set apart, because in them the referent of the word is the linguistic form of which the token is an exponent. The name in the other sentences might be glossed as follows:

2. '(the) person (I intended and expect you to identify) called *Thomas*'

3. 'member of the Thomas family (i.e., family called *Thomas*)'

4. 'particular aspect of Thomas (i.e., person called *Thomas*)'

5. 'person with some characteristics of a particular Thomas (i.e., person called *Thomas*)'

6. 'image of Thomas (i.e., person called *Thomas*)'

7. 'product of Thomas (i.e., person called *Thomas*)'

What all the glosses have in common is that they include either the word *Thomas* as a citation form or a term that must itself be so glossed. The examples therefore suggest that a proper name may be defined as a word whose definition includes a citation of the word itself. In the gloss for sentence (2), the citation form occurs as an element in a differentiating clause that directly modifies the genus, whereas in sentences (3) through (7) the citation form is an element in a clause that glosses some modifier of the genus. Names of the former kind can be called primary proper names, and those of the latter kind secondary proper names. Between these two sorts of names there are a number of differences in addition to the form of their glosses.

The bestowal of a primary proper name on a referent is ad hoc, in that there is no way to predict what primary name may be given to any particular referent. Consequently there is no way to know the correct use of primary names apart from observing instances of their use. Secondary names are bestowed according to rule and consequently their correct use does not depend on such observation. A speaker can know that a person is named *Catherine* only if he has heard or seen the name used in connection with her, and the initial decision to call her *Catherine* was an act of name-giving. On the other hand, if a speaker knows the name of the family to which an individual belongs, he will know what last name the individual bears without ever having heard or seen it used of the individual, and the initial application of the family name to the individual was not an act of name-giving at all because it follows automatically from general rules in our society. A family name is shared by the members of a family group and is regularly changed only by legal procedure, such as adoption or the marriage of females, as a concomitant of change of family membership. A family name is therefore primarily the name of the family group and only secondarily the name of an individual member.

Many secondary names have a tendency to pass easily into appellatives, so that whether a given use is proper or appellative may not be immediately clear. If we say, "Edinburgh was the Athens of Scotland," *Athens* is used as a secondary proper name meaning 'place with certain characteristics of Athens'; it will generally be understood as metaphorical, intended to call the original Athens to mind. However, if we say, "He is attending an academy," a metaphor is unlikely; the connection with the proper name *Academy* has faded, leaving the word as a pure appellative. Words continually move from the status of proper names, via secondary use, to the status of appellatives (see Partridge 1950 for examples). There may be doubt about the standing of a word that is in the process, for example *Casanova, Mata Hari,* or *Valentino,* and it is quite possible that for some speakers *Bluebeard* is a secondary proper name, derived from the Perrault character, while for others it is a simple appellative meaning 'uxoricide.'

The distinction between primary and secondary names is as "delicate" (in Halliday's sense) as it seems advisable to make. It would be easily possible to recognize more remote derivations. Thus *Israel* 'country called *Israel*' is a primary name; *Israeli* 'citizen of Israel (i.e., country called *Israel*)' is a secondary name; and *sabra* 'native-born Israeli (i.e., citizen of Israel (i.e., country called *Israel*))' would then be a tertiary name. Nothing prevents names being quarternary, quinary, and so on; however, the distinctions cease to have any practical significance. In common usage, primary and usually also secondary names are felt to be proper; tertiary (and higher degree derivations) are not. For practical purposes, a proper name can be said to be a word like *Thomas,* whose meaning is 'person called *Thomas*,' or like *Chicagoan,* whose meaning is 'inhabitant of the place called *Chicago*.' More generally, a proper name is primarily any word X whose meaning can be expressed as 'entity called X' and secondarily any whose immediate definientia include a term with such a meaning.

It may be objected that this schema for defining names is circular or involves infinite regression, on the grounds that the definition includes the term being defined (Brøndal 1948:60; Searle 1969:139). But the grounds are illusory and the objection invalid. The illusion of circularity is created by the appearance of the citation form X— whatever it may be, *Thomas,* for example—both as the definiendum and as part of the definiens. An examination of what is meant by "citation form" is therefore in order, followed by a more careful restatement of the definition schema for names.

Citation forms are used in a variety of ways. For example, we can say either "*Cat* is spelled with three letters" or "*Cat* has three letters," using the two statements interchangeably. However convenient it is to vary one's expression in this way, the two statements are not equivalent, strictly speaking, because the citation form *cat* stands for different things in the two uses. The first statement might be paraphrased as "{cat} is spelled with three letters," that is, the lexical formative or morpheme is represented by a three-letter spelling; the second statement as "<cat> has three letters," that is, the orthographic sequence is composed of three letters. The subjects are not interchangeable: "{cat} has three letters" is nonsense because morphemes are not composed of letters. We can also say things like "*Cat* is pronounced /kæt/," "*Cat* is a noun," "*Cat* means 'domestic feline,'" or "*Cat* is the genus 'feline' delimited by the differentia 'domestic,'" or any combination of such statements. By making all these statements about the same citation form *cat*, we seem to be saying that they are all true of the same entity. They are not. The citation form *cat* is a covering label, a fudge form, that can stand for any of several entities existing on different linguistic strata. To speak more precisely, we would have to make statements like the following:

> <cat>, which is the spelling for the morpheme {cat} and represents the pronunciation /kæt/, has three letters.

> /kæt/, which is the pronunciation of the morpheme {cat} and can be spelled <cat>, consists of three phonemes.

> {cat} is a noun, is pronounced /kæt/, is spelled <cat>, and means 'domestic feline.'

> 'cat' is a shorthand way of expressing the genus 'feline' and the differentia 'domestic,' which is the meaning of {cat}.

Normally, there is no harm in using the citation form *cat* as a cover term for any of <cat>, /kæt/, {cat}, or 'cat.' It is convenient typographically and lets us be looser with our wording than we would have to be if we were expressing ideas with greater exactness. If, however, we are misled by this loose practice to hypostatize a single entity behind the cover term, mischief may result. One possible bit of mischief is that the definition schema proposed above may be thought of as circular. If, however, we replace the citation form in that schema with more precise expressions, we have the following:

> The definition of any proper-name morpheme (sequence) {X} is 'entity (with such other differentiae as are appropriate) referred to in speech as /Y/ and in writing as <Z>.'

A specific example of the schema is the following:

> {Thomas} means 'person referred to in speech as /támǝs/ and in writing as <Thomas>.'

When the ambiguity represented by the citation form is eliminated from the definition, the vicious circularity disappears too.

It may also be objected that this approach to defining the proper name does not distinguish it from a common appellative (Ullmann 1952; Sørensen 1963:23). That is, if *Bill* means 'entity called *Bill*,' it is proposed that *boy* similarly means 'entity called *boy*.' But there is an important difference between the two sorts of words, and their meanings are not parallel. Suppose a strange animal wanders into my garden from the wilderness and I call out to my wife in the house, "There is a beast in our garden." Then she might ask, "Well, is it a cat, or an elephant, or a unicorn?" and I could reply, "It's a cat" or "None of those—it's an alligator." Though I had never seen the particular beast before, I would know whether it is or is not a cat. However, if my wife should ask instead, "Well, is it Macavity, or Pyewacket, or Caligula?" I would have to answer something like, "How should I know—we haven't been introduced yet." To know that a creature is appropriately referred to by the word *cat*, it is not necessary to observe anyone calling it "cat." But to know that the same creature is appropriately called *Pyewacket*, it is necessary to observe some instance of the use of that name with reference to the creature.

It is necessary to distinguish between the bestowal of a name and its subsequent use, a distinction that is not the same as that between the invention of an appellative neologism and its subsequent use. The invention (which can be taken here as including borrowing) of a new common word like *googol* or *sputnik* is parallel to the invention (or borrowing) of a new name like *Mauvenia* or *Rukmini*. The use of the appellative *sputnik* to refer appropriately to a particular object (an artificial satellite) is parallel to the use of *Rukmini* to refer appropriately to a particular person (a woman named *Rukmini*). But with names there is an event other than invention or use, an event that is not paralleled by anything connected with appellatives. Names are bestowed on particular individuals, and for a name to be associated with an individual, it is necessary that an act of bestowal should have taken place (Hockett 1958:311). Appellatives are invented and used; names are invented, bestowed, and used. The bestowal of a name may be deliberate, though informal, as when parents consider what name to give a new child; it may involve elaborate and extensive study, as when a public relations company gives a new name to a movie star; it may be off-hand, as when a child casually names a pet turtle. But in every case there is a specific act by which the name is first assigned to the bearer. There is no such act for appellatives. Appellatives are used but not bestowed; use of a name presupposes an act of bestowal. Thus the definition of a proper name *X* as 'entity called *X*' specifies not only a sufficient, but also a necessary condition for the correct application of the name. If the creature in my garden is a domestic feline, I will know that it is appropriately referred to by the word *cat* even though no one has ever before so referred to it. I cannot under similar circumstances know that it is to be called *Pyewacket*.

It is presumably this characteristic of the application of names that led Mill to conclude they are connotatively meaningless. However, Mill's conclusion goes too far by unnecessarily restricting what is to be accounted meaningful. What we are to understand by the term *meaning* is a vexed question. Gilbert Ryle (1957:128) has observed that "preoccupation with the theory of meaning could be described as the occupational disease of twentieth-century Anglo-Saxon and Austrian philosophy." It would be hubristic here to suggest any cure for the disease. But if we say that a word's meaning is a statement of the conditions necessary for its appropriate use, or as Ryle (1957:143) puts it, "to know what an expression means . . . is to know the rules of the employment of that expression," then no word can be meaningless. Just as part of one meaning of *cat* is that any possible referent be a domestic feline, so part of the meaning of *Pyewacket* is that any possible referent be in fact called *Pyewacket*. To be a cat it is not required that a creature ever in fact be so called; to be a Pyewacket, it is. Thus names and appellatives alike are meaningful words in the vocabulary, although their kinds of meaning differ.

The significant contrast between names and appellatives is not to be overlooked. In addition to the differences in the content of their definitions, names, unlike appellatives, are freely and imaginatively created de novo, as the colorful examples of personal names collected by Thomas Pyles (1947, 1959) attest. Moreover, the bestowal of names, whether traditional or innovative, is a prerogative of every speaker blessed with the possession of children, pets, boats, or other such nameables. It is hard for anyone to invent a new appellative and get his application of it accepted by others; but when it comes to names, every citizen is the equal of the primordial Name-giver of Plato's *Cratylus*. Also unlike the process of associating an appellative with a thing, the giving of names often involves a formal ceremony, a ritual or legal imposition, as in christenings, registrations, and launchings, which regularly include a performative utterance by which the name is made official: "Name this child. William Henry." Indeed appellatives are not "given" at all; they belong to a thing automatically by virtue of other characteristics it possesses. Names, however, are bestowed by someone, and only after that initial use in the act of bestowal do they become a characteristic of the subject to be observed by others and thus imitated.

It is also possible that names are governed by laws, synchronic and diachronic, that are different from those applying to appellatives (Mańczak 1968a, 1968b). Moreover, the name-stock of any language includes potentially the names of all other languages. Whereas appellatives are only exceptionally borrowed, the reverse is true for names. Names translated either as calques like *Red Square* and *Arch of Triumph* or as established native equivalents like *Leo* for *Lev* (Nikolaevich Tolstoi) are comparative rarities, the normal procedure being to accept the foreign name as a loan with whatever phonological, orthographical, and grammatical adaptations the borrowing language requires. So English has *The Hague* not *The Port*, *Vladivostok* not *Lordeast*, and *Juan Carlos* not *John Charles* for the Spanish royal person.

The grammar of names and appellatives is not altogether the same. It was noted in chapter 3 that the morphology of names need not follow that typical of nouns. In syntax, also, names have special characteristics. Thus, they alone occur in various naming constructions: *a man named Ishmael, Ishmael by name, of the name Ishmael,* and so forth. The earlier history of such constructions in Indo-European has been treated by Hahn (1969); something like them may be presumed to occur in all languages. They were studied at least as early as the fourteenth century, when Thomas of Erfurt recognized a class of expressions with a verbum vocativum in his modistic grammar (Bursill-Hall 1966:141). Some constructions of the type seem to admit either proper names or appellatives: "They called him Ishmael"; "They called him a rascal"; "They called him a sailor." However, the superficially similar constructions have quite different interpretations when a proper name and when an appellative is used in them. Thus it is a fact that the referent is Ishmael because he is so called; but it would be wrong to say (barring an extreme nominalist stance) that he is a rascal or a sailor because he is so called. In such constructions, names are used as citation forms and might be italicized or put in quotation marks, but appellatives do not normally have that interpretation; that is, in "Call me Ishmael," the word *Ishmael* is "mentioned," but in "Call me irresponsible," the word *irresponsible* is "used." Similarly, a sentence like "This is Golda" is ambiguous between two meanings: on the one hand, it may be an identification, with the sense 'This is the person Golda (whom I presume you know about)'; on the other, it may be an introduction, with the sense 'This person (whom I do not presume you to have any prior knowledge of) is called *Golda*.' With the first sense *Golda* is being used; with the second, mentioned. Appellatives occur with "introduction" meanings only in very restricted contexts, chiefly pedagogical, as when in a foreign language class, an instructor says, "This is a *kulero*, and this is a *telero*."

Such striking peculiarities mark names as a special kind of lexical item, but hardly exclude them from the realm of linguistic fact. Indeed, it may be said that there are three main kinds of vocables in the lexicon: those words that form closed systems in the grammar, such as the articles, pronouns, auxiliaries, and some prepositions and conjunctions; second, appellative nouns and those verbs, adjectives, and so forth that form open sets and constitute the bulk of words listed in general dictionaries; and last, names, which are often excluded from dictionaries on either theoretical or practical grounds. It is the contention of this study that there is no valid theoretical basis for excluding names from a dictionary, although their vast numbers and the small amount of linguistic information appropriate to each offer ample practical justification for leaving them out of general dictionaries. When dictionaries do include names, they tend to give encyclopedic rather than linguistic information about them, that is, they tend to discuss prominent persons or places named rather than the names themselves. There are exceptions, such as the "Pronouncing Vocabulary of Common English Given Names" appendix in the Merriam *New Collegiate* dictionaries. Fuller examples of appropriate lexicographical treatment of names are specialized works like Withycombe (1950) and Smith (1956); an early example is Walker (1818). On the other hand, a work like *Webster's Dictionary of Proper Names* (Payton 1970) is actually an encyclopedia of proper names, as are most works treating place names.

Names, whether considered lexically or referentially, are of many kinds, of which names of persons are the most central. Alone among nameable objects, persons are always assumed to have names. Whereas places, astronomical bodies, and events may be nameless, if we encounter an anonymous person, we ask about his name and if it is inaccessible, like Robinson Crusoe in his discovery of Friday, we supply the lack. Some entities, like animals and supernatural beings, will be expected to have names just in case they are treated as persons in other ways, such as requiring the relative *who* rather than *which*. Personal names are central in another way also. Although systems differ from culture to culture, it is common for a person to bear both primary and secondary names as part of a unified naming system. Other kinds of nameable objects seldom have names of both kinds.

Personal names are of two main sorts: legal names and bynames. Their kinds vary according to the naming system, some of whose manifold variations are noted by Lévi-Strauss (1966:172–216), but include given names (*Pollyanna, Timothy*), which are primary proper names, and secondary proper names such as patronymics (*Thorkelsdóttir, Ivanovich*) and family or clan names (*Jones, MacIntosh*). Some naming systems distinguish between an autonym, which is most like a given personal name in the English system, a teknonym, meaning 'father or mother of so-and-so,' and a necronym, which defines the individual's kinship to some deceased relative, for example, *Elder-brother-dead;* one person may have several such names that he bears serially according to the changing events of his life (Lévi-Strauss 1966:191–96). Bynames include hypocorisms (*Will, Bill, Jeannie*—although such apparent pet names can also occur as legal names), epithets used in addition to another name (*Stonewall Jackson, Jack the Ripper, Ethelred the Unready*) or in place of it (*Hotspur, Old Baldy*), code names (*M, 007*), noms de guerre (*Leclerc*—as for the general Vicomte de Hautecloque of the North African campaign), pen names (*George Sand*), stage names (*Engelbert Humperdinck*), aliases adopted for concealment (*John Smith*), and other pseudonyms (*Atticus*—as for Addison). Although they are grammatically common, descriptive phrases like *the Iron Duke, the Blessed Virgin, the Little Corporal, the White Queen,* and *the Lone Ranger* may be conventionalized in a way that makes them epithetic names. Bynames seem always to be primary proper names, even when they are based on secondary names. Thus the use of a hypocoristic form of a family name, such as *Jonesy,* is not predictable in the way the family name itself is and accordingly must be defined as a primary name.

A term for members of a group, organization, or community is a secondary proper name because the definition of the term will include reference to the name of the group. Thus names of nationalities like *Spaniard* can be defined as 'native or citizen of Spain (i.e., the country called *Spain*),' *Angle* as 'one of the Germanic tribe of Angles (i.e., the group called *Angles*),' *DeMolay* as 'member of the Order of DeMolay for Boys (i.e., the organization called *Order of DeMolay*),' and *mafioso* as 'member of the Mafia (i.e., the organization called *Mafia*).'

Titles, as well as some kinship and occupational terms, are regularly used with personal names, but are not themselves names since they can be defined without reference to their signaling value. Even when used alone as grammatically proper nouns, as in "Dad is in the closet where Momma hung him," "Doctor will see you now," or "Mister, you're next," such words are appellatives, not names. To know that a woman can be called *Madam*, it is not necessary to hear her so called.

The nonce use of expressions like *sleepyhead, big spender,* or *smartaleck* as proper nouns, for example in "See whether you can get sleepyhead to bed," does not imply that they are names, since an appellative definition will adequately account for the pseudo-name use. Personifications, as in Bunyan's "Wherefore *Mercy* began thus to reply to her Neighbor *Timorous*," are problematical. They function grammatically in every way like proper nouns, but they are probably best accounted appellatives rather than names, since the personification has the designation it does not merely because it is so called but because it is characterized by the quality signified by that designation.

A noteworthy item is *Joe Doakes*, which has two uses (apart from any occurrence as a genuine personal name, not under consideration here). First, it is used in the sense 'average, common man,' as in "Joe Doakes pays the taxes and fights the wars." Second, it is used with the sense 'person' of one whose name is unknown, as in "The next Joe Doakes who cuts in front is going to get a surprise." What is noteworthy about *Joe Doakes* is that it has all the associated characteristics of a name: it is capitalized, is syntactically a proper noun, and has the appearance of a hypocoristic given name plus a family name. However, in neither of the uses noted above is it a name. In both it is simply an appellative, as the glosses show. Indeed, *Joe Doakes* is the very antithesis of a name, for we can be reasonably confident that anyone of whom the term is used is not in fact called *Joe Doakes*. Moreover, users do not need to have observed an instance of its application to a person before knowing that it can be applied to him; rather *Joe Doakes* is used of a particular individual precisely when the speaker has not observed any use of his name, or it is used of a type, for which a name, in the strict sense, is not possible. *John Doe, Richard Roe, John Stiles,* and *Richard Miles* similarly are antinames, though with the added complication that they are used in the legal register in the general sense 'unnamed party to legal proceedings' and are further differentiated as the first, second, third, and fourth such parties. In effect, these terms constitute a special third-person pronoun system for the category "proximity." Like *Joe Doakes*, they are not names.

Names for nonpersons are less interesting onomastically because there is little variety in the kind of name, however much variety there may be in the things named. Names are given to places: eschatological realms (*Eden, Lotus Land*), astronomical bodies (*Aldebaran, Big Dipper, Venus*), topographical features of many kinds (*Fujiyama, Mississippi, Old Faithful, Sahara, Golden Horn, Heartbreak Ridge, Garden of the Gods, Gulf Stream, Micronesia, Okefenokee*), and political divisions (*Nepal, Danelaw, Ulster, Mohenjodaro, Cherokee Strip, Covent Garden, Portobello Road, Loop*).

Although the difference between proper names and appellatives is a discrete one, it is sometimes hard to decide whether a particular item is a name or not. Thus *Polaris* is an appellative if it is defined as the 'star most nearly aligned with the earth's axis over the north pole,' in which case, 12,000 years from now, as a result of the earth's precession, the star called Vega will be Polaris. On the other hand, *Polaris* is a name if, like *Regulus* or *Vega*, it is simply what a point of light is called. In the latter case, the fact that it was the polar star at the time it was named is a historical fact rather than a rule of usage.

Names are also given to historical events, whether their duration is brief or lasting: *Hegira, Children's Crusade, Glorious Revolution, Fifth Republic, Age of Reason,* and *Cenozoic Era,* for example. Place names are often used for events: *Vatican II,* before *Munich,* since *Kent State.* Many names of events are specialized uses of appellative phrases. Thus, *civil war,* as a common appellative, applies to any military conflict between sections or parties of the same nation; but the phrase can become conventionalized as the name for one or more particular historical events, such as the English Civil War of the 1640s or the American Civil War of the 1860s. The descriptive accuracy of the phrase is then no longer apposite. Indeed, in the case of the American conflict, the question of whether the war was a civil one or one between sovereign states was the immediate issue over which the war was fought. Despite the existence of alternative names of various descriptive implications, such as Horace Greeley's *Great Rebellion,* the United Daughters of the Confederacy's *War Between the States,* and a score of others recorded by McDavid and McDavid (1969), the appellative meaning of such expressions is largely irrelevant to their use as names. As witness to that irrelevance, there is a reference of the *New Orleans Times-Picayune* to the "Spanish War Between the States," cited by the McDavids as an amusing example of linguistic hyperdelicacy.

Whether *Monday* and other similar terms for recurring periods in the calendar are proper names has been the subject of much debate. Gardiner (1954:53–54), in a spirit of compromise, called them "common proper names," but the implications of such a *coincidentia oppositorum* are not altogether clear. If a definition like 'second day of the week' is appropriate for *Monday,* it is an appellative, as are the names of holidays, months, and seasons.

Many other things receive names: institutions and organizations (*Royal Academy, Republican Party, General Motors, NAACP, Yale, Dodgers*), beliefs and practices (*Islam, McCarthyism*), animals (*Checkers, Moby Dick*), plants (*Yggdrasil, Bo Tree, General Sherman Tree*), and gems (*Koh-i-noor, Cullinan*). Generic terms, whether English or Latin, popular or learned, are appellatives (*bald cypress, Taxodiaceae*). Artifacts are named: ships (*Pinafore*), trains (*Twentieth Century Limited*), aircraft (*Spirit of St. Louis*), spacecraft (*Odyssey*), weapons (*Hrunting*), buildings (*Alhambra, Madison Square Garden, Kremlin*), and various objects (*Holy Grail, Big Ben, Liberty Bell*).

Works of art customarily have titles as a special kind of name: books (*War and Peace*), periodicals (*Time*), comic strips (*Peanuts*), musical pieces (*Gaudeamus Igitur*), documents (*Tanaka Memorial*), plays (*The Tempest*), poems (*The Seasons*), paintings (*American Gothic*), prayers (*Angelus*), statuary (*Wingless Victory*), films (*The Great Dictator*), television programs (*All in the Family*), speeches (*Gettysburg Address*), and—although they are perhaps not works of art—laws, treaties, and the like (*Mann Act, Atlantic Pact*).

Names that are in fact used of only one referent, for example *Popocatepetl*, offer a problem in the form of their definition. As a name, the definition of *Popocatepetl* must be of the form 'entity (or perhaps more specifically, volcano) called *Popocatepetl*'; but because the word has unique reference, there is a possibility of defining it extensionally as 'volcano near Mexico City, 17,887 feet in height' or, more precisely, to include within the definition a location by the coordinates of longitude and latitude. There are practical difficulties in doing so. As Landau (1967:13) has observed, "no present grid system, or locating technique, can tell us precisely enough where most places on earth really are." Although we might conclude that language is imprecise enough to use imprecise coordinates, there are also theoretical objections to a definition that implies the volcano has the name *Popocatepetl* because of its location.

Similarly it might be supposed that the name of a particular person could be defined as referring to the individual begotten of such-and-such parents, at such-and-such a time, as Tristram Shandy was of Mr. and Mrs. Shandy in the ill-starred night between the first Sunday and the first Monday in the month of March, in the year of our Lord 1718. But the supposition is wrong, not merely because the same name can be given to more than one individual or because of practical difficulties in ascertaining the time and agents of begetting, but because so to define a name would imply that an individual has the name he does by virtue of the circumstances of his begetting. On the contrary, as is well-known, Tristram was so named because he was so called by the Reverend Mr. Yorick, in the face of the best parental intentions.

Extensional definitions, it has already been argued, are categorically wrong for linguistic purposes. They deal not with language, but with things. They are appropriate not for a grammar or dictionary, but for an encyclopedia. Language is used to talk about particulars; but within a language system, all terms are general terms.

An important, but still unanswered, question is what constitutes nameability, what properties a subject must possess in order to be eligible for a name. The requirement most often suggested is that the thing must be one that holds a special interest for speakers (Christophersen 1939:63; Russell 1948:89; Gardiner 1954:45; Pulgram 1954:32; Sørensen 1963:105; Waismann 1965:198; Zabeeh 1968:67). Chomsky (1971:14) suggests that nameability depends on the "function of an object in a space of human action," which is perhaps only another way of talking about "interest." It is clearly right that to be named, a thing must be something in which speakers might be interested, but that is a necessary rather than a sufficient condition. There are many things in which speakers have a reasonably strong degree of interest, such as a lawn that needs weekly mowing, a beefsteak on one's plate, or an antique firescreen. Yet outside fantasy, where all is possible, it would be exceedingly odd to call a lawn *Filbert*, a steak *Hank*, or a firescreen *Zoe*. The problem is not that the particular names are incompatible with their referents; it is rather that such referents do not get named, no matter how much interest we may have in them.

Another obviously necessary (but also insufficient) requirement is that the thing to be named must be recognizable as a gestalt. "Thing-ness" does not, however, require spatiotemporal continuity. As Chomsky (1971:14) points out, certain works of art, such as mobiles, are nameable although they lack spatial continuity; and the science-fictional James Kirk, transported from his spaceship to the surface of an alien planet, remains James Kirk although continuity is broken (the counterfactual nature of the example is irrelevant since the fiction is put forth not as fantasy, but as a reasonable possibility and is accepted as such by the audience).

A number of other criteria have been proposed: that names are given to entities so similar to one another that the differences between them are difficult to recognize or describe; that names are useful for entities that can serve as reference points for identifying other entities; that names, being economical means of referring, are given to objects for which such economy is desirable; and that names are given to things not susceptible to systematic ordering or for which standardized order seems inappropriate (Gardiner 1954: 45; Shwayder 1963:57). None of the foregoing are quite satisfactory criteria; and, indeed, it would be possible to argue for the exact opposites of the first and last.

There are also two sufficient, although not necessary, conditions for nameability: personhood and prominence. All persons are expected to have names; indeed an individual's name is bound up with his personhood, a nameless creature being thereby depersonalized. Nonhumans that are personalized are also usually named, for example, pets and supernatural powers. God's name may be ineffable, but he has one; the absolute which is unnamed is also impersonal.

Things that are prominent of their kind by virtue of intensity, size, duration, complexity, or whatnot are likewise nameable. Thus rivers have names, though the small creek flowing by my door has none. The clock at Westminster is *Big Ben*, but that in the local courthouse is anonymous. The *Star of India* is named, but not the stone in my wife's ring. Hurricanes are *Agnes, Beulah,* and the like, whereas tornados and summer storms are nameless. This criterion does not fully explain why some things are named and others not. Thus the event of 1666 when half the capital of England burned down is called the *Great Fire of London.* The event of 1945 when much of the city of Hiroshima was destroyed has no distinctive English name, although it can be described by various appellative phrases. How prominent a thing must be before it is named is subjective and partly a matter of chance.

Although the decision of whether to name or not to name is sometimes arbitrary or conventional, any subject that is either a person or exceptionally prominent of its kind is regularly given a name. And all named things may be presumed to be the objects of human interest and to have a gestalt-like cohesiveness. Beyond these criteria the requirements for nameability are not clear, although they are matters of some interest and may reasonably be supposed to be universals of human behavior.

The kind of definition that has been proposed here for proper names is not wholly new. It is implicit in Mill's (1843:1.2.5) observation that "when we predicate of anything its proper name, when we say, pointing to a man, this is Brown or Smith, or pointing to a city, that is York, we do not, merely by so doing, convey to the hearer any information about them, except that those are their names." Although Mill did not draw it, the obvious conclusion would seem to be that the information conveyed by a word is its meaning and therefore the meaning of a name is that the referent is so called. Marty (1908:438, 509) and Funke (1925:79) also noted this implication of the use of names, but it was Gardiner (1954) who recognized and most insistently called attention to the central role played by the "distinctive sound" of a name in its use. Gardiner's *Theory of Proper Names* is distorted by his almost exclusive attention to "embodied" proper names, that is, names with a definite referent in an act of parole—an ironic distortion in view of the fact that Gardiner was one of the chief proponents of Saussure's langue/parole distinction in England in the face of resistance to such dichotomizing by his contemporary J. R. Firth, who thought of it as "a quite unnecessary nuisance" (1957:144, 179, 227; Langendoen 1968:47). If we apply Gardiner's general theory to a consideration of "disembodied" names as units in the system of langue, a definition of the kind presented here follows naturally. With respect to ordinary language, Gardiner's work on names is the most important theoretical statement in recent times.

Another implicit recognition of the kind of meaning proposed here for names can be seen in Strawson (1950:188): "What is . . . implied . . . by my now referring to someone by name is simply the existence of someone, *now being referred to*, who is *conventionally referred to* by that name" (Strawson's italics). Although it is not true that the use of a name implies the existence of the referent (in the ordinary sense of *existence*), since fictional *Mrs. Miniver* is as good a name as historical *Mrs. Bracegirdle*, Strawson is certainly right that the referent may be assumed to be conventionally referred to by the name; it is this fact that the definition schema formalizes. Although Church (1956:5) did not himself limit the term so, he observed that *"proper name* is often restricted to names . . . which have as part of their meaning that the denotation is so called or is or was entitled to be so called." And according to Ryle (1931:27), when we understand a proper name, "we know that someone in particular is called by that name by certain persons." Zink (1963:491) similarly combines a so-und-so-genanntsein view of the meaning of names with an interpretation requiring them to have unique reference, when he proposes that "the meaning of a particular proper name 'P.N.' would be the meaning of the expression 'the person truly named "P.N." who is or was at the time T at place P.' " Although he puts most emphasis on the means by which a name is bestowed (as by christening or the inheritance of a patronym), Shwayder (1964:453) argues the use of a name "always implies that the speaker believes that the indicated denotatum has been given that name."

Finally, Bach (1968:92) wants "to postulate that all nouns (at least common nouns) are derived in one way, namely from structures of roughly the form

Det + one + S

where S is further developed into a sentence of the form

Det + one + Aux + be + Predicate nominal"

and subsequently he notes that "within the framework suggested here, names could be treated in two ways: They could be allowed to occur as alternatives to variables within sentences, or they could be derived from embedded sentences involving the predicate 'is called ——' or the like. If the latter course is followed, one could deal with the semantic content of names in a way parallel to that of other 'nouns' " (121). The first alternative follows the tradition of assuming that names have unique referents, which was argued against in chapter 4. The second, however, is the treatment that is advanced in this chapter as the most accurate statement of a name's meaning, in the sense of a rule that governs its use. It is also in keeping with the logical tradition of Russell (1905) and Quine (1950:220) that proposes to treat all singular terms as descriptions and to reanalyze descriptions as predications; in this tradition, too, all terms are general terms. Such a convergence of disciplines in their view of language is a welcome sign of the general usefulness of the analysis. Ordinary language and the predicate calculus may have a resemblance on the semantic level.

The approach to defining proper names in this chapter has several advantages that have not always been recognized:

1. It maintains that in respect to having meaning, proper names are normal words in the lexicon rather than peculiar "meaningless" words or extralinguistic phenomena. It normalizes proper names in this way because it regards their referents as belonging to intensional classes, like those of common nouns. In effect it says that Thomases are individuals who can be recognized by the fact that people apply the name *Thomas* to them, thus treating an individual's name like any other attribute by which he can be recognized and defined.

2. The form of the definition allows other attributes to be incorporated into it. If "A Boy Named Sue" is incongruous, the incongruity can be explained by a definition of the name *Sue* as a 'female person named *Sue*.' To the extent that names have connotations (in Mill's sense) those connotations can be included in their definitions, thereby also providing a partial explanation for the belief that proper and common names differ by degree. The necessary and sufficient condition for a proper name is that its definition be of the form 'entity called *X*'; if other information is included, for instance 'human' or 'female' or 'canine,' the name, while remaining categorically proper, becomes more common-like in its effect.

3. The distinction between primary and secondary proper names also formalizes the belief that proper and common names differ by degree rather than categorically. The formal difference between the meanings of primary names, like *Delilah* 'person called *Delilah*' or *Chicago* 'place called *Chicago*,' and those of secondary names, like a *Delilah* 'person with characteristics of a particular Delilah' or *Chicagoan* 'inhabitant of Chicago,' explains why there has been disagreement about whether items of the second kind are proper names, appellatives, or some sort of semiproper name.

4. On the other hand, the apparent circularity of the definition explains why Mill and others have thought names to be meaningless. If we are told we are to see a whale, we can confidently infer some things about the creature—that it is aquatic, warm-blooded,

and probably big. But if we are told we are to see Shome, all we can be sure of is that the entity can be called *Shome*. That is the meaning of the name, but it does not add much to our knowledge of the name-bearer. And consequently it is easy to conclude that names have no meaning.

5.   It has often been observed that users of a name must be supposed to know some facts about the named object that could be taken as the meaning of the name. But, as argued in chapter 4, if we take the sort of facts that are usually suggested as illustrations—that Aristotle was the student of Plato, or was the teacher of Alexander, or was born at Stagira—we have to conclude either that the meaning of a name is infinite, if we take the sum of those facts, or that it is indeterminate, if we take any part of them. There is, however, one fact about any referent that every namer of the referent must surely be assumed to know: that the referent is called by the name used in making reference; and it is this generally known fact that the definition specifies. Thus the position taken by those, like Frege, who believe a name to have some sense is also justified, but the definition makes that sense definite and describable, whereas otherwise it is not.

6.   The definition treats names as an autonomous and purely intralanguage semantic category. On the one hand, it escapes the problems that come from trying to base a definition on extra-linguistic reference; and on the other hand, it does not assume that the semantic class of names must be isomorphic with any grammatical, phonological, or orthographic classes. English has capitalized versus lowercase words in its orthography, proper versus common nouns in its grammar, and names versus appellatives in its semantics, but the various classes, though partly correlate, are independent of one another. In general, names are proper nouns and are capitalized, but exceptions are easy to find. In respect to naming, language would seem to be a multileveled and polysystemic phenomenon.

7.   Finally, the definition has, it would seem, a fair chance of being a universal of language. It is highly probable that all languages have words for which a necessary defining characteristic is that such a word can be applied to an entity just in case the entity is actually called by the word. Efforts to define a name orthographically, phonologically, or grammatically will end in language-specific phenomena that are of limited interest to the

general theory of onomastics; the name as a universal is a semantic category.

A name is therefore a word people use to call someone or something by. So we may conclude that Hermogenes was right after all, and Cratylus wrong. If people called him *Hermogenes*, that was his name, because what a man is called is, after all, what a name is.

References

Ashley, Leonard R. N. 1971. "Changing Times and Changing Names: Reasons, Regulations, and Rights." *Names* 19:167–87.

Austin, J. L. 1961. "The Meaning of a Word." In *Philosophy and Ordinary Language*, ed. Charles E. Caton, pp. 1–21. Urbana: University of Illinois Press, 1963.

Ayer, A. J. 1963. *The Concept of a Person, and Other Essays.* New York: St. Martin.

Bach, Emmon. 1968. "Nouns and Noun Phrases." In *Universals in Linguistic Theory*, eds. Emmon Bach and Robert T. Harms, pp. 90–122. New York: Holt.

Berle, Alf K., and de Camp, L. Sprague. 1959. *Inventions, Patents, and Their Management.* Princeton, N.J.: Van Nostrand.

Bloomfield, Leonard. 1933. *Language.* New York: Holt.

Bolinger, Dwight. 1971. *The Phrasal Verb in English.* Cambridge: Harvard University Press.

————. 1972. "Accent is Predictable (If You're a Mind-Reader)." *Language* 48:633–44.

Bowman, William Dodgson. 1931. *The Story of Surnames.* London: Routledge.

Bréal, Michel Jules A. 1897. *Essai de sémantique—science des significations.* Paris: Hachette.

Brøndal, Viggo. 1948. *Les Parties du discours: études sur les catégories linguistiques.* Traduction française par Pierre Naert. Copenhagen: Einar Munksgaard.

Brown, Goold. 1851. *The Grammar of English Grammars.* Reprint. New York: William Wood, 1873.

Bursill-Hall, Geoffrey. 1966. "Aspects of Modistic Grammar." In *Report of the Seventeenth Annual Round Table Meeting of Linguistics and Language Studies*, ed. Francis P. Dinneen, pp. 133–48. Monograph Series on Languages and Linguistics, no. 19. Washington: Georgetown University Press.

Carroll, Lewis. 1871. *Through the Looking-Glass, and What Alice Found There.* In *The Annotated Alice*, ed. Martin Gardner, pp. 166–345. New York: Clarkson N. Potter, 1960.

Chafe, Wallace L. 1970. *Meaning and the Structure of Language.* Chicago: University of Chicago Press.

Chomsky, Noam. 1965. *Aspects of the Theory of Syntax.* Cambridge: MIT Press.

————. 1971. *Problems of Knowledge and Freedom.* New York: Random House.

Christophersen, Paul. 1939. *The Articles: A Study of Their Use in English.* Copenhagen: Einar Munksgaard.

Church, Alonzo. 1956. *Introduction to Mathematical Logic*. Princeton: Princeton University Press.

Collinson, William Edward. 1937. *Indication: A Study of Demonstratives, Articles, and other 'Indicaters.'* Language Monographs, no. 17. Baltimore: Waverly.

Coseriu, Eugenio. 1967. "El plural en los nombres proprios." In *Teoria del lenguaje y linguistica general: cinco estudios*, pp. 261–81. 2d ed. Madrid: Editorial Gredos.

Curme, George O. 1935. *Parts of Speech and Accidence*. Boston: Heath.

Dallas, James. 1913. "The Honorific 'The.'" *Scottish Historical Review* 10:39–46. Comment by Herbert Maxwell, ibid., pp. 230–31.

Davidson, Thomas. 1874. "The Grammar of Dionysios Thrax." *Journal of Speculative Philosophy* 8:326–39.

DeCamp, David. 1967. "African Day-Names in Jamaica." *Language* 43:139–47.

Der-Houssikian, Haig. 1970. "Definiteness and Indefiniteness." Manuscript.

Dillard, J. L. 1968. "On the Grammar of Afro-American Naming Practices." *Names* 16:230–37.

Donald, Henderson H. 1952. *The Negro Freedman*. New York: Schuman.

Dykema, Karl W. 1972. "Anglicized Forms of Proper Names: A Report on a Questionnaire Filled Out by Students at Youngstown State University." In *Studies in Linguistics in Honor of Raven I. McDavid, Jr.*, ed. Lawrence M. Davis, pp. 359–65. University, Ala.: University of Alabama Press.

Feldman, Harold. 1959. "The Problem of Personal Names as a Universal Element in Culture." *American Imago* 16:237–50.

Firth, J. R. 1957. *Papers in Linguistics, 1934–1951*. London: Oxford University Press.

Frege, Gottlob. 1892. "On Sense and Reference." In *Translations from the Philosophical Writings of Gottlob Frege*, eds. Peter Geach and Max Black, pp. 56–78. Oxford: Blackwell.

Funke, O. 1925. "Zum Definition des Begriffes 'Eigenname.'" In *Probleme der englischen Sprache und Kultur*, Festschrift für Johannes Hoops. Germanische Bibliothek, Abt. 2, Bd. 20.

Gardiner, Alan. 1951. *The Theory of Speech and Language*. 2d ed. Oxford: Clarendon.

————. 1954. *The Theory of Proper Names*. 2d ed. London: Oxford University Press. First printed in 1940.

Gleason, H. A., Jr. 1965. *Linguistics and English Grammar*. New York: Holt.

Gove, Philip B. 1965. "The Nonlexical and the Encyclopedic." *Names* 13:103–15.

Green, William. 1972. "Humorous Characters and Attributive Names in Shakespeare's Plays." *Names* 20:157–65.

Hacking, Ian. 1968. "A Language without Particulars." *Mind* 77:168–85.

Hahn, E. Adelaide. 1969. *Naming-Constructions in Some Indo-European Languages*. Cleveland: Case Western Reserve University Press.

Halliday, M. A. K. 1961. "Categories of the Theory of Grammar." *Word* 17:241–92.

————. 1967–68. "Notes on Transitivity and Theme in English." *Journal of Linguistics* 3:37–81, 199–244; 4:179–215.

Hamp, Eric P. 1956. Review of *Theory of Names*, by Ernst Pulgram. *Romance Philology* 9:346–50.

Harms, Robert T. 1968. *Introduction to Phonological Theory*. Englewood Cliffs, N.J.: Prentice-Hall.

Harris, James. 1751. *Hermes; or, A Philosophical Inquiry Concerning Language and Universal Grammar.* Reprint. Menston, Yorkshire: Scolar Press, 1968.

Hill, Archibald A. 1958. *Introduction to Linguistic Structures.* New York: Harcourt.

———. 1966. "A Re-Examination of the English Articles." In *Report of the Seventeenth Annual Round Table Meeting on Linguistics and Language Studies,* ed. Francis P. Dinneen, pp. 217–31. Monograph Series on Languages and Linguistics, no. 19. Washington: Georgetown University Press.

Hockett, Charles F. 1958. *A Course in Modern Linguistics.* New York: Macmillan.

Householder, Fred W. 1971. *Linguistic Speculations.* Cambridge: At the University Press.

Jacobs, Roderick A., and Rosenbaum, Peter S. 1968. *English Transformational Grammar.* Waltham, Mass.: Blaisdell.

Jakobson, Roman. 1972. "Verbal Communication." *Scientific American* 227 (September):73–80.

Jespersen, Otto. 1909–49. *A Modern English Grammar on Historical Principles.* 7 vols. Copenhagen: Einar Munksgaard.

———. 1922. *Language: Its Nature, Development, and Origin.* London: Allen and Unwin.

———. 1924. *The Philosophy of Grammar.* Reprint. New York: Norton, 1965.

Johnson, W. E. 1921. *Logic.* Reprint. New York: Dover, 1964.

Jowett, B. 1873. *The Dialogues of Plato.* 4 vols. New York: Scribner.

Keil, Heinrich. 1864. *Grammatici Latini.* 8 vols. Reprint. Hildesheim: Olm, 1961.

Krapp, George Philip. 1925. *The English Language in America.* New York: Century.

Kruisinga, E. 1932. *A Handbook of Present-Day English.* 5th ed. 4 vols. Groningen: Noordhoff.

Lakoff, George. 1971. Foreword to *Where the Rules Fail,* by Ann Borkin et al. Ann Arbor: Department of Linguistics, University of Michigan. Mimeographed.

Lamb, Sydney M. 1966. *Outline of Stratificational Grammar.* Washington: Georgetown University Press.

[Lancelot, Claude, and Arnauld, Antoine.] 1660. *Grammaire générale et raisonnée.* Reprint. Menston, Yorkshire: Scolar Press, 1968.

Landau, Robert M. (357–03–6623). 1967. "Name or Number—Which Shall It Be?" *Names* 15:12–20.

Langendoen, D. Terence. 1968. *The London School of Linguistics: A Study of the Linguistic Theories of B. Malinowski and J. R. Firth.* Research Monograph, no. 46. Cambridge: MIT Press.

———. 1970. *Essentials of English Grammar.* New York: Holt.

Leech, Geoffrey N. 1969. *Towards a Semantic Description of English.* London: Longmans.

Lévi-Strauss, Claude. 1966. *The Savage Mind.* Chicago: University of Chicago Press.

Linsky, Leonard. 1963. "Reference and Referents." In *Philosophy and Ordinary Language,* ed. Charles E. Caton, pp. 74–89. Urbana: University of Illinois Press.

Long, Ralph B. 1961. *The Sentence and its Parts.* Chicago: University of Chicago Press.

92   ON DEFINING THE PROPER NAME

————. 1969. "The Grammar of English Proper Names." *Names* 17:107–26.
Lyons, John. 1966. "Towards a 'Notional' Theory of the 'Parts of Speech.'" *Journal of Linguistics* 2:209–36.
Manual of Style. 1969. 12th ed. Chicago: University of Chicago Press.
Mańczak, Witold. 1968a. "Le Nom propre et le nom commun." *Revue Internationale d'Onomastique* 20:205–18.
————. 1968b. "Onomastik und Strukturalismus." *Beiträge zur Namenforschung* 3:52–60.
Marty, Anton. 1908. *Untersuchungen zur Grundlegung der allgemeinen Grammatik und Sprachphilosophie.* Vol. 1. Halle: Max Niemeyer.
Matthews, C. M. 1966. *English Surnames.* London: Weidenfeld and Nicolson.
McCawley, James D. 1968. "The Role of Semantics in a Grammar." In *Universals in Linguistic Theory,* eds. Emmon Bach and Robert T. Harms, pp. 124–69. New York: Holt.
McDavid, Raven I., and McDavid, Virginia G. 1969. "The Late Unpleasantness: Folk Names for the Civil War." *Southern Speech Journal* 34:194–204.
McMillan, James B. 1949. "Observations on American Place-Name Grammar." *American Speech* 24:241–48.
Merton, Robert K. 1965. *On the Shoulders of Giants: A Shandean Postscript.* New York: Harcourt.
Michael, Ian. 1970. *English Grammatical Categories and the Tradition to 1800.* Cambridge: At the University Press.
Mill, John Stuart. 1843. *A System of Logic.* Reprint. New York: Harper, 1846.
Morris, Charles. 1946. *Signs, Language, and Behavior.* Reprint. New York: George Braziller, 1955.
Mullally, Joseph P. 1945. *The Summulae Logicales of Peter of Spain.* Publications in Mediaeval Studies, no. 8. Notre Dame, Ind.: University of Notre Dame Press.
Müller, F. Max. 1891. *The Science of Language.* Vol. 1. New York: Scribner.
Palmer, Harold E., and Blandford, F. G. 1969. *A Grammar of Spoken English.* 3d ed., rev. Roger Kingdon. Cambridge, England: Heffer.
Partridge, Eric. 1950. *Name into Word: Proper Names that Have Become Common Property.* New York: Macmillan.
Payton, Geoffrey. 1970. *Webster's Dictionary of Proper Names.* Springfield, Mass.: Merriam.
Postal, Paul. 1966. "On So-Called 'Pronouns' in English." In *Modern Studies in English,* eds. David A. Reibel and Sanford A. Schane. Englewood Cliffs, N.J.: Prentice-Hall, 1969.
Poutsma, H. 1914. *A Grammar of Late Modern English.* 4 vols. Groningen: Noordhoff.
Prenner, Manuel. 1942. "Ora Jones Married Ora Jones." *American Speech* 17:84–88.
Pulgram, Ernst. 1954. *Theory of Names.* Berkeley: American Name Society. Reprint from *Beiträge zur Namenforschung,* vol. 5, no. 2.
Pyles, Thomas. 1947. "Onomastic Individualism in Oklahoma." *American Speech* 22:257–64.
————. 1959. "Bible Belt Onomastics; or, Some Curiosities of Anti-Pedobaptist Nomenclature." *Names* 7:84–100.
Quine, Willard Van Orman. 1950. *Methods of Logic.* New York: Holt.
————. 1960. *Word and Object.* Cambridge: MIT Press.
————. 1963. *From a Logical Point of View.* New York: Harper.
Quirk, Randolph; Greenbaum, Sidney; Leech, Geoffrey; and Svartvik, Jan. 1972. *A Grammar of Contemporary English.* London: Longmans.

Rennick, Robert M. 1970. "The Nazi Name Decrees of the Nineteen Thirties." *Names* 18:65–88.
Roberts, Paul. 1967. *Modern Grammar*. New York: Harcourt.
Robins, R. H. 1966. "The Development of the Word Class System of the European Grammatical Tradition." *Foundations of Language* 2:3–19.
———. 1967. *A Short History of Linguistics*. Bloomington: Indiana University Press.
Robinson, Fred C. 1972. "Appropriate Naming in English Literature." *Names* 20:131–37.
Russell, Bertrand. 1905. "On Denoting." *Mind* 14:479–93.
———. 1918. "The Philosophy of Logical Atomism." *The Monist* 28:509–27.
———. 1919. *Introduction to Mathematical Philosophy*. London: Allen and Unwin.
———. 1940. *An Inquiry into Meaning and Truth*. New York: Norton.
———. 1948. *Human Knowledge: Its Scope and Limits*. New York: Simon and Schuster.
Ryle, Gilbert. 1931. "Systematically Misleading Expressions." In *Logic and Language*, ed. Antony Flew, pp. 13–40. Garden City, N.Y.: Doubleday, 1965.
———. 1953. "Ordinary Language." In *Philosophy and Ordinary Language*, ed. Charles E. Caton, pp. 108–27. Urbana: University of Illinois Press, 1963.
———. 1957. "The Theory of Meaning." In *Philosophy and Ordinary Language*, ed. Charles E. Caton, pp. 128–53. Urbana: University of Illinois Press, 1963.
Sampson, Geoffrey. 1970. "Towards a Linguistic Theory of Reference." Typescript.
Searle, John R. 1958. "Proper Names." *Mind* 67:166–73.
———. 1969. "The Problem of Proper Names." In *Semantics—An Interdisciplinary Reader in Philosophy, Linguistics, and Psychology*, eds. Danny D. Steinberg and Leon A. Jakobovits, pp. 134–41. Cambridge: At the University Press, 1971.
Shwayder, D. S. 1963. *Modes of Referring and the Problem of Universals: An Essay in Metaphysics*. University of California Publications in Philosophy, no. 35. Berkeley: University of California Press.
———. 1964. Review of *The Meaning of Proper Names*, by H. S. Sørensen. *Journal of Philosophy* 61:450–57.
Sledd, James. 1959. *A Short Introduction to English Grammar*. Chicago: Scott, Foresman.
Sloat, Clarence. 1969. "Proper Nouns in English." *Language* 45:26–30.
Smith, Carlota S. 1964. "Determiners and Relative Clauses in a Generative Grammar of English." *Language* 40:37–52.
Smith, Elsdon C. 1956. *Dictionary of American Family Names*. New York: Harper.
———. 1966. "The Significance of Name Study." In *Proceedings of the Eighth International Congress of Onomastic Sciences*, ed. D. P. Blok. Janua Linguarum, Series Major 17. The Hague: Mouton.
———. 1969. "Influences in Change of Name." *Onoma* 14:158–64.
Sørensen, Holger Steen. 1958. *Word-Classes in Modern English with Special Reference to Proper Names*. Copenhagen: Gad.
———. 1963. *The Meaning of Proper Names*. Copenhagen: Gad.
Stageberg, Norman C. 1971. *Introductory English Grammar*. 2d ed. New York: Holt.
Stockwell, Robert P.; Schachter, Paul; and Partee, Barbara Hall. 1968. *Inte-

gration of Transformational Theories on English Syntax. Electronic Systems Division USAF TR 68–419. Los Angeles: University of California.

Strang, Barbara M. H. 1968. *Modern English Structure.* 2d ed. New York: St. Martin's. First published in 1962.

Strawson, P. F. 1950. "On Referring." In *Philosophy and Ordinary Language,* ed. Charles E. Caton, pp. 162–93. Urbana: University of Illinois Press, 1963.

————. 1959. *Individuals: An Essay in Descriptive Metaphysics.* London: Methuen.

Sweet, Henry. 1891. *A New English Grammar.* 2 vols. Reprint. Oxford: Clarendon, 1960.

Togeby, Knud. 1951. *Structure immanente de la langue française.* Travaux du Cercle Linguistique de Copenhague, no. 6. Reprint. Paris: Larousse, 1965.

Ullmann, S. 1952. Review of *Theory of Proper Names,* by Alan Gardiner. *Archivum Linguisticum* 4:66–67.

Utley, Francis Lee. 1963. "The Linguistic Component of Onomastics." *Names* 11:145–76.

Varro, Marcus Terentius. 1964. *De Lingua Latina,* eds. G. Goetz and F. Schoell. Amsterdam: Hakkert.

Vendler, Zeno. 1967. *Linguistics in Philosophy.* Ithaca: Cornell University Press.

Waismann, F. 1965. *The Principles of Linguistic Philosophy,* ed. R. Harré. New York: St. Martin's.

Walker, John. 1818. *A Key to the Classical Pronunciation of Greek, Latin, and Scriptural Proper Names.* New York: Collins and Hannay.

Wells, Rulon. 1954. "Meaning and Use." In *Theory of Meaning,* eds. Adrienne and Keith Lehrer, pp. 113–35. Englewood Cliffs, N.J.: Prentice-Hall, 1970.

Withycombe, E. G. 1950. *The Oxford Dictionary of English Christian Names.* Oxford: Clarendon.

Witkowski, Teodolius. 1964. *Grundbegriffe der Namenkunde.* Deutsche Akademie der Wissenschaften zu Berlin Vorträge und Schriften, no. 91. Berlin: Akademie-Verlag.

Wolf-Rottkay, W. H. 1971. "Some Onomastic and Toponomastic Aspects of Icelandic Traditionalism." *Names* 19:229–39.

Zabeeh, Farhang. 1968. *What Is in a Name? An Inquiry into the Semantics and Pragmatics of Proper Names.* The Hague: Nijhoff.

Zandvoort, R. W. 1969. *A Handbook of English Grammar.* 5th ed. London: Longmans.

Zink, Sidney. 1963. "The Meaning of Proper Names." *Mind* 72:481–99.

Zinkin, Vivian. 1969. "The Syntax of Place-Names." *Names* 17:181–98.

UNIVERSITY OF FLORIDA MONOGRAPHS

Humanities

No. 1: *Uncollected Letters of James Gates Percival,* edited by Harry R. Warfel

No. 2: *Leigh Hunt's Autobiography: The Earliest Sketches,* edited by Stephen F. Fogle

No. 3: *Pause Patterns in Elizabethan and Jacobean Drama,* by Ants Oras

No. 4: *Rhetoric and American Poetry of the Early National Period,* by Gordon E. Bigelow

No. 5: *The Background of* The Princess Casamassima, by W. H. Tilley

No. 6: *Indian Sculpture in the John and Mable Ringling Museum of Art,* by Roy C. Craven, Jr.

No. 7: *The Cestus. A Mask,* edited by Thomas B. Stroup

No. 8: *Tamburlaine, Part I, and Its Audience,* by Frank B. Fieler

No. 9: *The Case of John Darrell: Minister and Exorcist,* by Corinne Holt Rickert

No. 10: *Reflections of the Civil War in Southern Humor,* by Wade H. Hall

No. 11: *Charles Dodgson, Semeiotician,* by Daniel F. Kirk

No. 12: *Three Middle English Religious Poems,* edited by R. H. Bowers

No. 13: *The Existentialism of Miguel de Unamuno,* by José Huertas-Jourda

No. 14: *Four Spiritual Crises in Mid-Century American Fiction,* by Robert Detweiler

No. 15: *Style and Society in German Literary Expressionism,* by Egbert Krispyn

No. 16: *The Reach of Art: A Study in the Prosody of Pope,* by Jacob H. Adler

No. 17: *Malraux, Sartre, and Aragon as Political Novelists,* by Catharine Savage

No. 18: *Las Guerras Carlistas y el Reinado Isabelino en la Obra de Ramón del Valle-Inclán,* por María Dolores Lado

No. 19: *Diderot's* Vie de Sénèque: *A Swan Song Revised,* by Douglas A. Bonneville

No. 20: *Blank Verse and Chronology in Milton,* by Ants Oras

No. 21: *Milton's Elisions,* by Robert O. Evans

No. 22: *Prayer in Sixteenth-Century England,* by Faye L. Kelly

No. 23: *The Strangers: The Tragic World of Tristan L'Hermite,* by Claude K. Abraham

No. 24: *Dramatic Uses of Biblical Allusion in Marlowe and Shakespeare,* by James H. Sims

No. 25: *Doubt and Dogma in Maria Edgeworth,* by Mark D. Hawthorne

No. 26: *The Masses of Francesco Soriano,* by S. Philip Kniseley

No. 27: *Love as Death in* The Iceman Cometh, *by Winifred Dusenbury Frazer*

No. 28: *Melville and Authority,* by Nicholas Canaday, Jr.

No. 29: *Don Quixote: Hero or Fool? A Study in Narrative Technique,* by John J. Allen

No. 30: *Ideal and Reality in the Fictional Narratives of Théophile Gautier,* by Albert B. Smith

No. 31: *Negritude as a Theme in the Poetry of the Portuguese-Speaking World,* by Richard A. Preto-Rodas

No. 32: *The Criticism of Photography as Art: The Photographs of Jerry Uelsmann,* by John L. Ward

No. 33: *The Kingdom of God in the Synoptic Tradition,* by Richard H. Hiers

No. 34: *Dante Gabriel Rossetti's Versecraft,* by Joseph F. Vogel

No. 35: *T. S. Eliot's Concept of Language: A Study of Its Development,* by Harry T. Antrim

No. 36: *The Consolatio Genre in Medieval English Literature,* by Michael H. Means

No. 37: *Melville's Angles of Vision,* by A. Carl Bredahl, Jr.

No. 38: *The Historical Jesus and the Kingdom of God,* by Richard H. Hiers

No. 39: *In Adam's Garden: A Study of John Clare's Pre-Asylum Poetry,* by Janet M. Todd

No. 40: *Democracy, Stoicism, and Education: An Essay in the History of Freedom and Reason,* by Robert R. Sherman

No. 41: *On Defining the Proper Name,* by John Algeo